HOUSTON GOURMET COOKS 2

Exciting recipes from 21 of Houston's finest restaurants

by
Ann Criswell

Foreword – Maxine Mesinger
Columnist Houston Chronicle
Illustrations – Ken Boehnert

Publisher – Fran Fauntleroy

Acknowledgments

Foreword by Maxine Mesinger
Columnist *Houston Chronicle*

Cover and illustrations – Ken Boehnert

Back cover photograph – Ed Daniels

Design – Larry Knapp

Setting for back cover – The Jamail Family Market

Flowers – The Party Artists

Printing – Gulf Printing

Houston Gourmet Cooks
Houston, Texas

Copyright ©1988 by Houston Gourmet
All rights reserved. No portion of this book may be reproduced without written permission from the publisher.

Printed in the United States of America

ISBN 0-9613643-5-1

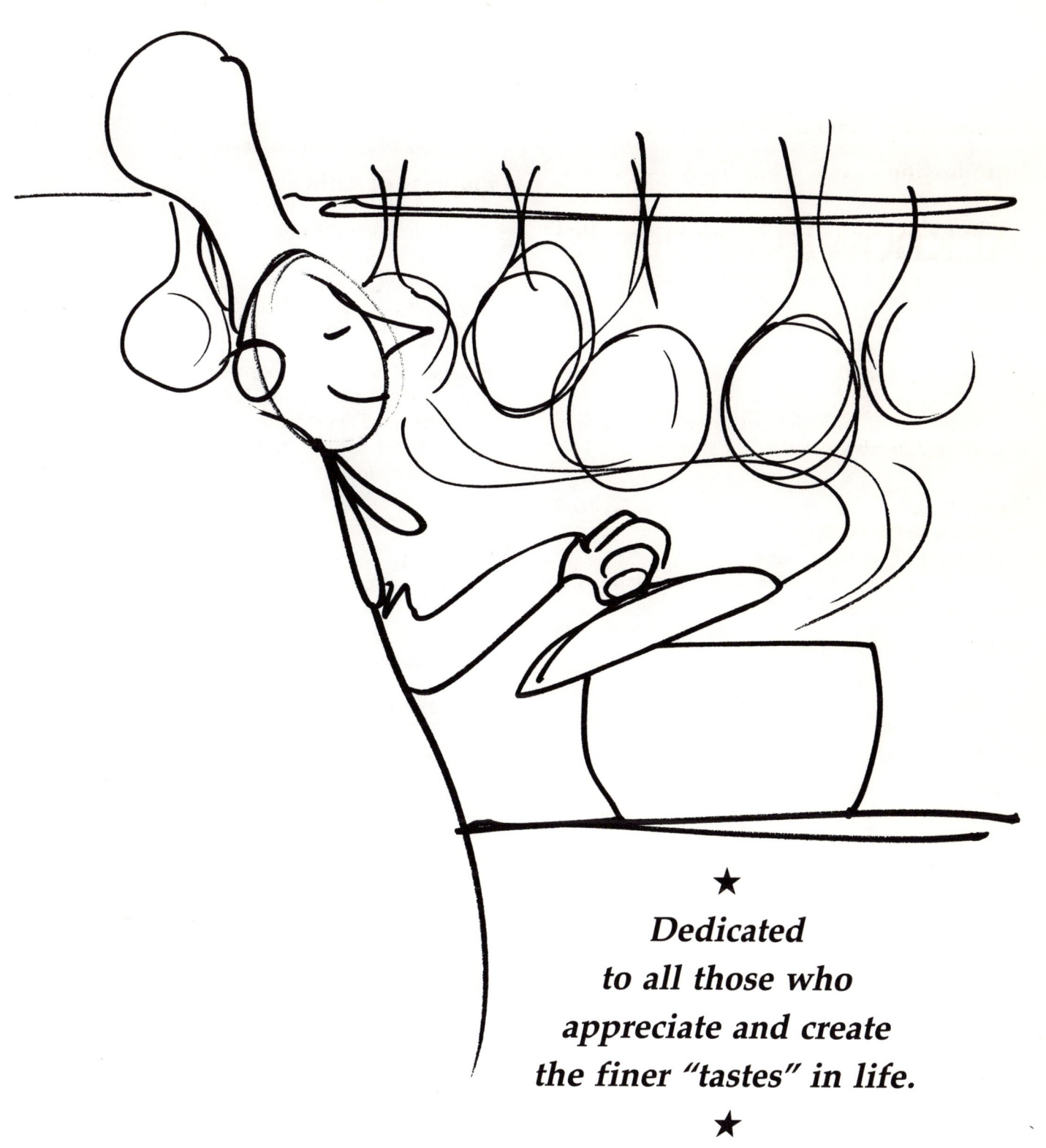

★
*Dedicated
to all those who
appreciate and create
the finer "tastes" in life.*
★

Contents ★★★

Foreword by Maxine Mesinger 8

Introduction 9

Anthony's 10-15
    Cucumber Dill Soup
    Tomatoes Anthony With Pecan Vinaigrette
        Dressing
    Avocado Mousse With Crab and Dijon Vinaigrette
    Green and White Pasta Primavera
    Lemon Sole With Mustard, Breadcrumbs, Chives,
        Tomatoes and Basil
    Veal Pancetta With Mascarpone and Pancetta Sauce
    White Chocolate Mousse Anthony

Brennan's 16-21
    Jalapeno Cheese Soup
    Grilled Fresh Tuna Salad
    Gulf Shrimp With Crispy Rice Cakes and Creole
        Meuniere Sauce
    Beef Tenderloin on a Bed of Sweet Onions With
        Creole Mustard Sauce
    Creole Succotash Timbales
    Mile High Mud Pie With Warm Chocolate
        Sauce

Cafe Adobe/Austin's 22-25
    Chicken Taco Salad
    Shrimp Enchiladas With Ranchero Sauce
    Mexican Pizza
    Sopabananapilla
    Austin's Seafood Stuffed Mushrooms
    Austin's Meatloaf
    Austin's Texas Brownie Pie

Cavatore's 26-29
    Spinaci con Mozzarella
        (Spinach With Mozzarella Cheese)
    Fettucini Pescatore
        (Fettucini With Seafood)
    Pollo Arrosto al Rosmarino
        (Breast of Chicken With Rosemary)
    Vitello con Scallops Bianchina
        (Veal and Sea Scallops Bianchina)
    Melanzane Parmigiana
        (Eggplant Parmesan With Marinara Sauce)
    Cafe Cavatore

DeVille (Four Seasons-Houston Center) . 30-35
    Smoked Lamb Nachos, Poached Tortilla Chips,
        Refried Black Beans and Pico de Gallo
    Campfire Salmon With Braised Fennel
    Charcoaled Axis Venison With Grilled Summer
        Vegetables and Red Bell Pepper Sauce
    Low-Cal Green Apple and Jicama Slaw
    Seven Grain Bread
    Cobbler of Peaches, Basil and Cherries With
        Southern Comfort Sauce

Empress of China 36-39
    Avocado Shrimp With Tangy and Spicy Sauce
    Karbar Beef Strings
    Sesame Scallops
    Sand on the Snow
    Peking Roasted Chicken
    Broccoli in Special Garlic Sauce

Hunan River/Red Pepper 40-43
    Four Delight of King Pao
    Imperial Two Flavors
    Steamed Scallops and Vegetables
    Broccoli in Garlic Sauce
    Red Pepper's Dry Sauteed String Beans
    Red Pepper's Shrimp Fried Rice

Kim Son 44-47
    Spring Rolls (Goi Cuon)
    Salted Crabs With Black Pepper
    Charcoal Broiled Beef With Lemon Grass
    Vietnamese French Coffee

La Reserve 48-51
    Chilled Artichoke Soup
    Spring Salad With Boursin Wontons
    Poached Flouder With Peppercorn Cream Sauce
    Chicken With Green Asparagus Coulis
    Medallions of Lamb With Three Mushrooms
        and Basil Sauce
    Lemon Tart

La Tour d'Argent 52-55
    Gratin de Queues de Crevettes aux Champignons
        Sauvages Nouilles Fraiches
        (Gratin of Shrimp With Wild Mushrooms and
        Fresh Noodles)
    Saute de Faisan aux Abricots Secs a la Creme
        (Pheasant With Dried Apricots and Cream Sauce)
    Medaillons de Veaux aux Endives a la Creme
        de Gingembre
        (Veal Medallions With Endive and Ginger)
    Salade Frisee au Crotin de Chavignol
        (Curly Endive With Goat Cheese)
    Asperges Sauce Mousseline
        (Asparagus With Mousseline Sauce)
    Flambees de Bananes Martiniquaise
        (Flamed Bananas Martinique-Style)

Les Continents/The Brasserie 56-59
    Earl Grey Sour
    Kiwi Ginger Sparkle
    Fillet of Redfish Wrapped in Lettuce Leaves
    Baby Chicken Mercado With Cilantro Lime Butter
    Beef Tenderloin Tips in Green Peppercorn Cream
       Sauce With Garlic Fried Rice
    Glazed Strawberry Dessert Soup
    Strawberry Cheesecake

Louisiana Don's 60-63
    Snapper Courtbouillon
    Crawfish Etouffee
    Shrimp and Avocado Salad
    Cajun Stuffed Pork Roast
    Blueberry Cheesecake
    Louisiana Meringue Bread Pudding

Prego 64-67
    Roasted Poblano Crab Cakes With Lemon Caper
       Tomato Mayonnaise
    Grilled Chicken Salad
    South of the Border Fettucini With Grilled
       Chicken and Black Beans
    Summery Linguini With Black Beans, Corn,
       Cilantro and Tomato Sauce for Two
    Grilled Lamb Chops With Pink Peppercorn Sauce

Quail Hollow Inn 68-71
    Chinese Chicken Salad With Honey Ginger
       Dressing
    Flounder With Lime
    Quail With Apples
    Quail Hunters Delicacy
    Cheesecake

Rao's Ristorante Italiano & Bar ... 72-75
    Radicchio and Fennel Salad
    Tony Rao's Risotto
    Involtini de Pollo
    Snapper Toto
    Ravioli al Sugo

Remington on Post Oak Park 76-79
    Maryland She Crab Soup With Thyme
    Grilled Chicken Caesar Salad
    Warm Spinach Salad With Pancetta Bacon and
       Sherry Vinaigrette
    Stir-Fried Duck With Oriental Vegetables and
       Sesame Pasta
    Seared Gulf Red Snapper With Mint Marigold
       Sauce and Three Salsas (Mango Black Bean
       Salsa, Yellow Bell Pepper Tomato Salsa and
       Jicama Tomatillo Salsa)

Rudi Lechner's 80-83
    White Wine Cheese Soup
    Crepe Hubert
    Chicken Breast Southern California
    Calf Liver With Red Onion-Apple Butter Sauce
    Zucchini Nut Bread

Thai Cafe 84-87
    Nam Sodd
       (Ground Pork Appetizer)
    Thai Satay With Cucumber Salad
    Thom Ka Gai
       (Coconut Chicken Soup)
    Papaya Salad
    Beef With Sweet Basil
    Stir-Fried Vegetables
    Sticky Rice and Mango
    Thai Tea

Tony's 88-91
    Swordfish Salad
    Eggplant Terrine
    Poussin (Baby Chicken) Framboise
    Breast of Chicken With Peppercorns
    Braciole alla Napoletana
    Apple Tart Tony's

Tony Mandola's 92-95
    Ceviche
    Shrimp Cocktail Vicente
    Deviled Crab/Crab Balls
    Red Beans, Sausage and Rice
    Seafood Lasagna
    Tony Mandola's Bread Puddin' With
       Whiskey Sauce

Vargo's 96-99
    Cheese Spread
    Shrimp Scampi
    Veal Scallopini al Marsala
    Vargo's Special Filet
    Chicken alla Romana
    Chocolate Roll

Special Helps 100-102
    Brown Sauce
    Stocks (Beef, Chicken, Fish)

Shopping Guide 102-104

Index 105-109

About Ann Criswell 109

Who's Who Houston Gourmet Cooks . 110

Foreword

by Maxine Mesinger

Being one of that rare breed, a native Houstonian, I have watched with amazement the growth of the city's restaurants through the years, especially the past 30 years or so.

In the 1950s Houstonians going to New York City talked a lot about looking forward to the dining out experiences there.

I heard it said over and over that one could get any kind of food in the world right in little ol' New York. There was an abundance of Chinese, Italian, French, Russian, American steak houses, ad infinitum. There were, and probably still are, more wonderful delis in New York than anywhere in the world.

In those days, too, if you wanted a good Maine lobster, blue point oysters or clams, you had to go east to get them. Very few were flown to Houston as regular fare at our local restaurants. What a change hath been wrought here!

These days, Houstonians have their choice of myriad fast food houses, chains that have sprung up all over the country. But we can also choose from the finest in American regional, French, Italian, Chinese, Vietnamese, Thai, Mexican or Tex-Mex, Indian and seafood from the Gulf or from the eastern seaboard. We have wonderful soul food restaurants where we can dress casually, and we have restaurants which are as elegant as any you'll find in New York—or Paris, for that matter.

Because there is such a wide variety of dine-out choices and because the restaurants are scattered over all parts of the city, it's hard to know where to go without some sort of guide.

All of us are guilty of getting into a rut and going to the same places time after time, simply because we don't want to take chances on unfamiliar new places.

Then along came Ann Criswell, one of Houston's leading food authorities and cookbook authors. Ann, who has been food editor of the Houston Chronicle for 22 years, has dined in most of the restaurants in Houston and has passed on recipes from many of them via the Chronicle and her books.

Her recent book, "Houston Gourmet Cooks", was such a hit that she has brought us "Houston Gourmet Cooks 2." It offers us recipes from 21 of Houston's finest restaurants. All the recipes are new and so are the restaurants, with the exception of Brennan's, La Tour d'Argent and La Reserve in Inn on the Park.

The recipes cover a wide range of international cuisines, to suit whatever dining, or cooking, mood you are in. So, browse the book, then go out on the town and "graze" in Houston's vast collection of restaurants.

This book does the ground work for you—there are descriptions of the restaurants, lists of their best features and tested recipes.

All you have to do is enjoy.

Introduction

"Houston Gourmet Cooks 2," a cookbook with a whole new menu of restaurant recipes, is like second helpings of "Houston Gourmet Cooks."

A few of our favorite restaurants, sadly, have left the scene since "Houston Gourmet Cooks" was published last year, but many more restaurants have opened, and we have added many new discoveries to our list of favorites.

Choices of restaurants and recipes reflect the trends; because Asian cuisines are growing in popularity, you will notice more Oriental recipes in "Houston Gourmet Cooks 2."

Houston is developing a real love for Vietnamese, Chinese, Thai, Japanese, Korean and other Far Eastern cuisines, and restaurants are springing up on every corner and in every shopping center to satisfy this culinary curiosity. Along with the restaurants come "boutique" food shops that provide the exotic ingredients— from fiery chili pastes to passion fruit.

Browsing through the aromatic aisles of international supermarkets has become a leisure-time activity in itself. Grocery shopping is a weekend obsession for leisure-time cooks who want to be the first to try new tastes.

The number of Italian restaurants that have opened in the past year indicates that Italian food is a major trend here. Southwestern food with its blue cornmeal, chilies and flavorful salsas, continues to increase in popularity, and Cajun, Middle Eastern, American (especially southern) and Indian cuisines have strong followings.

The fun is in the experimenting. We borrow something from one cuisine and add it to another. We discover that pico de gallo is a fine relish for black-eyed peas or that the flavors of grilled smoked chicken and honey mustard give new taste dimensions to chicken salad.

Not all the trendy restaurants are exotic. Houston also is rediscovering the joys of simple cooking—a perfectly roasted chicken, real mashed potatoes, meatloaf and bread pudding have everyday appeal.

We are also increasingly concerned about healthful eating. Better restaurants share this concern and are accommodating their cooking and choice of ingredients to guidelines set by major health organizations such as the American Heart Association and American Cancer Society. If you prefer polyunsaturated margarine to butter, skim milk to whole, broiled or roasted meats and fish to fried, make your wishes known.

Houston restaurateurs are incredibly creative. Some of the recipes in this book are as simple as milk; others require more expertise, and you will want to practice them before springing them on guests.

The restaurants and chefs realize that home cooks will take liberties and shortcuts with their recipes. After all, few of us make our own stocks, brown sauce and reductions, and few can afford crab, lobster, shrimp, veal, cream and expensive cheeses on a day-to-day basis.

However, the integrity and quality of the ingredients are the most significant factors in the success of many dishes, so make substitutions thoughtfully. Check the Special Helps and Shopping Guide sections at the back of this book for useful information and sources for ingredients.

Here are some of the ingredients the chefs and restaurateurs in this book consider important: fresh produce, meats, fish and herbs; extra-virgin olive oil and flavored oils; clarified butter; heavy cream (at least 36 percent milkfat); high-quality pasta, whether fresh or dried; good vinegar; shallots; lemon zest (the thinnest yellow part of the peel only); Roma tomatoes (the deep red, teardrop-shaped Italian tomatoes); jicama; black beans, and a variety of chilies and mushrooms.

Have fun reading and cooking from "Houston Gourmet Cooks 2" and continue to enjoy the changing tastes of Houston.

—**Ann Criswell**

Anthony's

FAVORITES

Cucumber Dill Soup

Tomatoes Anthony With Pecan Vinaigrette

*Avocado Mousse Topped With Crab,
Tomato & Dijon Sauces*

Green and White Pasta Primavera

*Lemon Sole With Mustard, Breadcrumbs,
Chives, Tomatoes & Basil*

Veal Pancetta

White Chocolate Mousse Anthony

Anthony's is the epitome of the "today" restaurant—chic but casual, convivial but not clubby, food that is imaginative but not intimidating.

In only three years, it has become a fixture on the Inside-the-Loop dining scene and earned critical acclaim including a one-star rating from Texas Monthly magazine.

The decor sets the casual mood—a color scheme of salmon pink, blues, grays and beige, terra cotta tile floors; square, turquoise-canopied windows; stenciled ceiling borders; eclectic art work and fresh flowers everywhere. The dining room looks out on the fountain courtyard of Chelsea Market, which has the ambiance of a small European market place.

Art work was personally selected by owner Tony Vallone, and waiters can provide a hand-drawn guide that maps the location of works by Allan Otto Smith, Groff, Rabel, Rector and Douglas Semi Van.

Food becomes part of the decor in the ever-changing antipasto table at the entrance to the dining room. The antique table holds an assortment of antipasto dishes in colorful Italian pottery containers. The display whets your appetite for the delicacies to come—deep-fried sausage balls with horseradish sauce (served as a complimentary starter), eggplant appetizers, peppers, olives, sausages, salami and cheeses.

If your favorite "appetizer" is people watching, you're in luck. There is a constant parade of notables from the social, business and arts worlds because of Anthony's proximity to River Oaks, the Montrose area museums and art galleries, University of St. Thomas, Rothko Chapel and Texas Medical Center.

If you are in search of a drink or light meal before or after the theater or art exhibit opening, or supper after racquetball or tennis, you're in luck again. Anthony's opens for dinner at 5:30 p.m. (Sundays, too) and offers soups, salads and appetizer portions of pasta dishes. They are particularly appropriate for light dining or quick meals. You can drop in, but reservations are requested to get you out on time for the theater or museum tour.

Anthony's menu is basically Italian, but is as eclectic as the art work. Stuffed artichokes, Chicken Nonna (named for Tony Vallone's grandmother) and redfish happily co-exist on the menu with upscale arugula salad with goat cheese and raspberry vinaigrette, Fedelini Ralph (a rich pasta dish with mascarpone cheese, broccoli and porcini mushrooms named for managing partner Ralph Cook) and rabbit roasted with red and yellow peppers and wild mushrooms.

Tony Vallone's wife Donna makes the popular Italian regine cookies.

Star Attractions

★ Italian dining with contemporary flair—fine pasta dishes, seafood and veal. Menu specialties such as baby artichokes in a garlicky breading, cucumber dill soup, homemade potato chips, grilled crab cakes and a variety of exceptional veal dishes. Menu changes seasonally.

★ Convenient hours for dining before or after the theater, concert or social event: 5:30 to 11 p.m. Monday through Thursdays; to 11:30 p.m. Fridays and Saturdays and to 9:30 p.m. Sundays. Lunch hours: 11:30 a.m. to 2 p.m.

★ Full-service bar that seats 30 to 40.

★ Excellent wine list specializing in Italian and California selections.

★ Special orders prepared with 24-hour notice.

★ Dessert cart featuring tiramisu (the Italian mascarpone cheese-ladyfinger-custard dessert), ricotta angel food cake with fresh strawberry sauce and coconut amaretto sponge cake. The piece de (least) resistance is Chocolate Seven Layer Cake, a multi-layer confection of chocolate mousse, cake and whipped cream. It's the house birthday cake.

★ Upbeat atmosphere, casual dress code (you'll see mostly coats and ties and dresses, but some diners come in designer shorts).

Cucumber Dill Soup

- ½ cup (1 small) diced white onion
- ¼ cup soft butter
- 5 cucumbers peeled, seeded and chopped
- Dash of bottled hot red pepper sauce
- 1½ cups chicken stock
- Juice of 2 lemons
- 2 tablespoons chopped garlic
- ½ cup chopped fresh dill
- 1 cup whipping cream
- Salt and pepper
- 1 cucumber, peeled and sliced very thin for garnish
- Fresh dill sprigs for garnish

In a large saucepan, saute onion in butter until golden brown. Add the cucumbers and simmer 5 minutes. Add pepper sauce, chicken stock, lemon juice, garlic and dill.

Process in food processor or blender until smooth. Chill. Stir in cream and adjust seasoning.

Ladle into chilled cups. Garnish with sliced cucumber and dill sprigs.

Serves 4.

Tomatoes Anthony

2 heads radicchio
1 head Boston Bibb lettuce
8 peeled tomato slices
4 fresh artichoke hearts, cooked in seasoned water or chicken stock with lemon until tender
4 hearts of palm
1 bunch watercress, washed, patted dry and trimmed
4 tablespoons minced tomatoes
Pecan Vinaigrette Dressing (recipe follows)

On a salad plate, arrange radicchio leaves and lettuce. Arrange tomatoes on lettuce. Garnish with artichoke hearts, hearts of palm, watercress and minced tomatoes. Serve with Pecan Vinaigrette Dressing.

Serves 4.

Pecan Vinaigrette Dressing

4 ounces toasted pecans
1 tablespoon sugar
1 cup salad oil
¼ cup red wine vinegar
1 ounce white wine Worcestershire sauce
1 teaspoon bottled hot pepper sauce
1 tablespoon Dijon mustard
¼ teaspoon each salt and black pepper

Place pecans, sugar, oil, vinegar, Worcestershire, pepper sauce, mustard, salt and pepper in food processor and process until blended thoroughly. Pour over Tomatoes Anthony.

Note: See Special Helps section for method for toasting pecans.

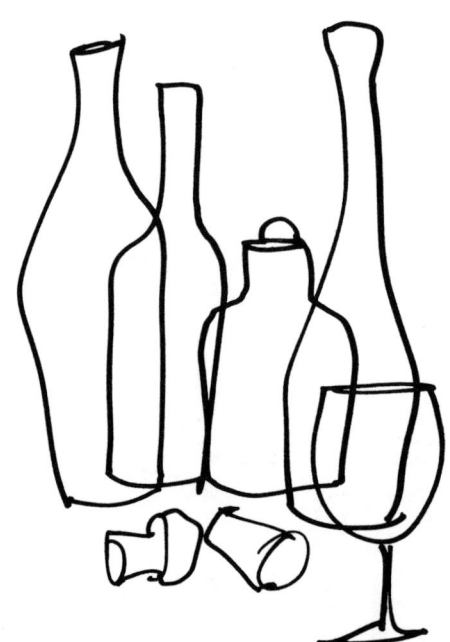

Avocado Mousse

- 2 tablespoons minced garlic
- 2 tablespoons minced shallots
- 1 tablespoon olive oil
- 3 avocados, peeled, seeded and cut in chunks
- 1 tablespoon minced basil leaves
- 1 tablespoon minced chives
- 3 tablespoons minced green onion
- 1 cup chopped leaf spinach
- 1 tablespoon crushed whole coriander
- 1 tablespoon bottled hot pepper sauce
- 2 tablespoons Worcestershire sauce
  Salt and pepper to taste
- 1 envelope unflavored gelatin powder, dissolved in ¼ cup cold water
- ½ cup whipping cream, whipped to a soft peak
  Dijon Vinaigrette (recipe follows)
- 4 ounces jumbo lump crabmeat
- 4 tablespoons diced tomato

In skillet, saute garlic and shallots in olive oil over medium heat 2 to 3 minutes. Let cool.

Combine avocado, basil, chives, green onion, spinach, coriander, pepper sauce, Worcestershire, salt, pepper, garlic and shallots in food processor. Pulse until mixture is smooth. Remove and place in stainless steel bowl.

Line a 9x5x3-inch loaf pan with clear plastic wrap. Mix dissolved gelatin into avocado mixture; fold in cream. Place mixture into pan and cover with plastic wrap. Chill until firm, 2 to 3 hours.

Dijon Vinaigrette
- 2 tablespoons minced shallots
- 2 tablespoons minced garlic
- 1 tablespoon olive oil
- 6 tablespoons salad oil
- 2 tablespoons cider vinegar
- 1 tablespoon white wine
  Salt and pepper

Saute shallots and garlic in 1 tablespoon olive oil in skillet over medium heat 2 to 3 minutes. Place in food processor and blend in remaining oil, vinegar and white wine. Process until blended. Season with salt and pepper.

To serve: Spoon Dijon Vinaigrette onto serving platter, slice avocado mousse and place on vinaigrette. Top with crabmeat and diced tomato.

Serves 4.

Green and White Pasta Primavera (Paglia e Fieno Primavera)

- 4 ounces each green and white fettucini

Alfredo Sauce
- 4 ounces soft unsalted butter
- 4 tablespoons minced garlic
- 3 cups heavy (whipping) cream
- 6 ounces freshly grated Parmesan cheese
  Salt and ground black pepper
  Seasonal Vegetables: 1 ounce each steamed broccoli, yellow beans, sugar snap peas, cauliflower, julienne of red and yellow bell peppers and sliced mushrooms.
- 2 tablespoons olive oil

Bring salted water to a boil in 3-quart pot. Add pasta and cook al dente. Remove, drain and reserve.

Make Alfredo Sauce. Melt butter in saucepan over medium heat and saute garlic, stirring 1 to 2 minutes. Add cream. Simmer liquid until reduced by half. Stir in cheese. Adjust seasoning with salt and pepper. Remove from heat and set aside.

Add sliced vegetables to boiling water; simmer 2 to 3 minutes. Remove. In saucepan toss pasta with olive oil. Add sauce and vegetables; stir to mix with serving spoon or tongs. Divide pasta into bowls. Spoon vegetables and sauce over pasta and serve.

Serves 4.

Lemon Sole With Mustard, Breadcrumbs, Chives, Tomatoes and Basil

- 4 (6-to 8-ounce) sole fillets
- 4 teaspoons Dijon mustard
- Salt and pepper
- 4 teaspoons Italian breadcrumbs
- 1 tablespoon each minced garlic and shallots
- 1 ounce olive oil
- 1 cup heavy whipping cream
- 2 cups diced Roma tomatoes
- ¼ cup fresh chopped basil
- 2 tablespoons chopped chives

Brush sole fillets with Dijon mustard. Season with salt and pepper. Sprinkle with breadcrumbs. Bake at 350 degrees 10 to 12 minutes.

For sauce: In a saucepan over medium heat, saute garlic with shallots in oil. Simmer 1 minute, add the cream and reduce to a sauce consistency, about half. Stir in the tomatoes, basil and chives. Spoon sauce on plate. Arrange sole fillets over sauce and serve.

Serves 4.

Veal Pancetta

- Mascarpone and Pancetta Sauce (recipe follows)
- 2 tablespoons clarified butter
- 8 veal scallopini
- Salt, ground white pepper and flour

Prepare sauce.

Heat butter in saute pan over medium heat. Season veal with salt and pepper and lightly dust with flour. Saute veal about 30 seconds per side. Remove and arrange on serving plates.

Mascarpone and Pancetta Sauce
- 2 tablespoons finely chopped pancetta (Italian bacon)
- ½ teaspoon each minced shallots and garlic
- 2 tablespoons heavy (whipping) cream
- 3 tablespoons mascarpone cheese (Italian fresh double cream cheese; preferably Gambia)
- ¼ cup sliced fresh mushrooms
- ¼ cup diced peeled, seeded tomatoes
- 1 tablespoon chopped fresh basil leaves
- Salt and pepper if needed

Add pancetta to saute pan; cook until crispy. Drain off excess fat and reserve pancetta. Add shallots and garlic to the pan and saute over medium heat 1 minute.

Add cream and mascarpone. Reduce by half to sauce consistency. Add mushrooms, tomatoes and basil stirring with a spoon to incorporate into sauce. Bring mixture to a boil. Adjust seasoning.

Reheat veal scallopini and spoon sauce over it on serving plates. Arrange mushrooms on top. Garnish with diced tomatoes tossed with a little olive oil and chopped garlic. Serve with sauteed eggplant.

Serves 2.

White Chocolate Mousse Anthony

- 6 ounces white chocolate
- ¼ cup milk
- 1 ounce cream of coconut (such as Coco Lopez)
- 1 ounce creme de cacao
- 2 extra large eggs, separated
- Pinch of salt
- 1 cup whipping cream (chill cream, bowl and beaters well)

Place white chocolate and milk in a stainless steel bowl. Melt in a double boiler over simmering water (or melt in microwave on 50 percent power; stir to smooth). Remove from heat and add cream of coconut and creme de cacao.

In a mixing bowl beat egg whites to a soft peak and add the pinch of salt. In another bowl, whip the cream to a soft peak.

Assemble by folding half the cream into chocolate mixture. Fold remaining cream into the egg whites, then fold chocolate mixture into egg whites. Refrigerate and allow to set 2 to 3 hours before serving.

Serves 4.

Note: Skillful pastry cooks may want to serve the mousse in a cookie shell basket as it is in the restaurant. There the mousse is beautifully presented in a caramelized hazelnut cookie shell with caramel sauce overall. The shells are so delicate that the pastry chef only makes a few at a time an hour or so before they are served so they won't disintegrate in Houston's humidity.

Anthony's
4611 Montrose
Houston, Texas 77006
524-1922

Brennan's

FAVORITES

Jalapeno Cheese Soup
Grilled Fresh Tuna Salad
Gulf Shrimp With Crispy Rice Cakes
Beef Tenderloin on a Bed of Sweet Onions
With Creole Mustard Sauce
Creole Succotash Timbale
Mile High Mud Pie
With Warm Chocolate Sauce

Brennan's is a Houston tradition for many reasons. We go there on weekends for fun—the Saturday Jazz Brunch with Dixieland band or quieter Sunday brunch is a great way to entertain friends, family or out-of-town guests.

Or we go to celebrate life's rites of passage—a birthday, job promotion, engagement or anniversary. During the past 21 years, the fountain patio and Garden Room have been the setting for innumerable engagement parties, weddings, wedding receptions and anniversaries.

Or we go to enjoy great food. Brennan's unique Texas Creole Cuisine is coming of age under the direction of the current generation of the Brennan restaurant family, cousins Alex Brennan-Martin and Dick Brennan Jr., who say they learned to make a roux before they learned to ride a bike.

They are weaving the Creole classics of New Orleans into the fabric of such "today" menu items as Texas Venison Hash, mesquite grilled ribeye with grilled onions, poblano peppers and tortilla strips, and Eggs St. Charles—poached eggs on crisp-fried trout fillets with a tomatillo hollandaise.

Although most customers would never completely forsake Brennan's originals such as Trout With Roasted Pecans, Veal Chop Tchoupitoulas and Creole Bread Pudding Souffle, more and more are tempted by the tantalizing tastes of new dishes.

Houston also appreciates the Brennans for their civic-mindedness, especially for their support of the arts such as the Alley Theatre and Houston Grand Opera.

Star Attractions

★ Texas Creole Cuisine—the best traditional regional ingredients used in creative new ways.

★ Romantic atmosphere—shady patio with fountain, flowers, hanging baskets and twinkle lights in the trees.

★ Creative interiors by Alex Brennan-Martin's wife, Christine. She hand-placed the taupe and pink Portuguese marble tiles in the dining room, and with artist Jane Bazinet hand-painted canvas for wall coverings and flat Roman shades to match the marble. Complementary paintings were personally selected by Adelaide Brennan.

★ The Garden Room has been redecorated with new floral carpet, peach, burgundy and forest green, chairs in burgundy leather snakeskin pattern and trompe l'oeil painting on connecting doors.

★ Noteworthy building (one-time home of the Houston Junior League). It was designed by John Staub, the renowned architect of Houston's posh River Oaks section.

★ LiteStyle Cuisine. Creative low-calorie dishes such as Smoked Chicken Gumbo, Chilled Poached Spicy Oranges and Chilled Grilled Shrimp and Peppers.

★ Dramatic Combination—Dinner at Brennan's and tickets for a performance at the Alley Theatre for the price of the meal alone.

★ One of the city's best and largest wine lists—strong on California wines, Bordeaux and Burgundies.

★ Awards—Brennan's of Houston was awarded Restaurant Business magazine's Executive Dining Award in 1985 as one of the top 100 restaurants in the U.S. and Canada, received the prestigious Restaurant Institutions magazine Ivy Award in 1983 and has received the Travel Holiday award consistently since the

1970s. The restaurant also is one of American Express' Platinum Card Preferred Welcome restaurants.

★ Special dessert menu featuring Brennan's strawberry shortcake, Mile High Mud Pie, Creme Brulee and Creole Bread Pudding Souffle, hand-made ice creams, dessert wines, Cognacs, coffees and liqueurs.

★ Fresh herbs from a kitchen garden including mint for Brennan's unique marinated mint juleps.

★ Complimentary praline for each departing guest (lagniappe, that little something extra that is so typical of New Orleans hospitality).

Jalapeno Cheese Soup

2	tablespoons butter
¼	cup finely chopped celery
¼	cup finely chopped green bell pepper
½	cup finely chopped yellow onion
1	quart rich chicken stock
½	cup roux (recipe follows)
1	pound grated Jalapeno pepper cheese
1	tablespoon Worcestershire sauce
1	tablespoon hot sauce (see Note)
1	teaspoon chopped garlic
½	cup heavy (whipping) cream
	Ground black pepper to taste
	Salt as needed
	Red Pepper Puree (recipe follows)

Note: In any recipe that calls for hot sauce, you can use bottled red pepper sauce or Louisiana hot sauce interchangeably. Brennan's recommends Crystal's Louisiana hot sauce from New Orleans.

Heat large saucepan and melt butter. Add chopped celery, bell pepper and onion and cook, with pan partially covered, until vegetables "sweat."

Add chicken stock and bring to a simmer. Whisk in enough roux to give the soup a little body, about ½ cup. Gradually add grated cheese, letting it melt in before adding more.

Add Worcestershire, pepper sauce and garlic. Whisk in cream.

If the soup gets too thick, add a little more chicken broth. Season to taste with salt and pepper. Garnish with Red Pepper Puree (see Peppers in Special Helps section for roasting instructions).

Roux

Heat 4 ounces (½ cup) clarified butter in saucepan; whisk in 4 ounces (about 1 cup) all-purpose flour. Cook, whisking constantly, 5 to 10 minutes, until roux is golden brown.

Red Pepper Puree

Remove skin and seeds from 1 roasted red bell pepper. Puree in electric blender with a little chicken stock.

Diet Alert: Use defatted, low-sodium chicken stock and part-skim milk jalapeno cheese and substitute lighter cream, half-and-half or milk for heavy cream.

Gulf Shrimp With Crispy Rice Cakes

- 28 raw shrimp, cleaned and butterflied
- 4 tablespoons butter
- 1½ teaspoons minced garlic
- 3 teaspoons finely chopped shallots
- 6 ounces sliced mushrooms
- 3 ounces (about 1 bunch) green onion, sliced
- 6 tablespoons finely diced fresh tomato
- 3 teaspoons seafood seasoning (such as Creole Cravings)
- 4 teaspoons white wine
- 4 tablespoons Worcestershire sauce
- 2 tablespoons Louisiana hot sauce
- ¼ cup heavy (whipping) cream
- ½ cup Creole Meuniere Sauce (recipe follows)
- Crispy Rice Cakes (recipe follows)

Melt butter in hot saute pan. Add garlic and shallots and saute a minute or 2 to develop the flavors, but do not brown.

Add shrimp, mushrooms, green onion, tomato and seasoning. Cook a minute, then add the white wine, Worcestershire, hot sauce and cream. Saute until the shrimp is almost done, then add the Meuniere sauce.

To serve: Arrange 2 Crispy Rice Cakes on plate and spoon shrimp and sauce over them.

Serves 4.

Creole Meuniere Sauce

- 1 quart veal or beef stock
- Pulp and juice of 1½ lemons
- ¼ cup hot sauce
- ¼ cup Worcestershire sauce
- 1½ sticks unsalted butter, cut in cubes
- Salt and pepper as needed
- ¼ cup roux (see Note)

Combine stock, lemon pulp and juice, pepper sauce and Worcestershire in a saucepot. Over medium heat, simmer until reduced by half. Whisking constantly, stir in roux and cook about 5 minutes over medium heat.

Remove from heat and whisk in butter. Season with salt and pepper.

Note: Make roux with 2 ounces flour (about ½ cup) and 2 ounces (4 tablespoons) clarified butter. See Roux in Special Helps section.

Crispy Rice Cakes

- 3 tablespoons butter
- 2 tablespoons each finely chopped celery, red bell pepper and yellow onion
- ½ teaspoon finely chopped garlic
- 2 cups cooked rice
- 2 tablespoons thinly sliced green onion
- 1 tablespoon Worcestershire sauce
- ½ tablespoon (1½ teaspoons) bottled red pepper sauce
- 1 tablespoon soy sauce
- 1 egg, beaten
- ½ cup dry bread crumbs
- Salt and pepper as needed

Melt butter in saute pan and saute celery, pepper, onion and garlic.

Stir in rice, green onion, Worcestershire, pepper sauce and soy sauce. Cook about 1 more minute, then remove from heat. Add egg, mixing well; work quickly and don't let egg curdle.

Add enough bread crumbs to lighten the mixture, and season to taste with salt and pepper. Form 8 (1-inch thick) patties and refrigerate until completely chilled.

When ready to serve, saute in clarified butter.

Serves 4.

Grilled Fresh Tuna Salad

This is Brennan's fresh tuna version of Salade Nicoise.

- 12 ounces fresh tuna steak
  Salt and white pepper to taste
- 6 small new red potatoes (with skins), boiled and diced
- 3 haricots vert (tiny thin French green beans), blanched
- 2 Roma tomatoes, diced (teardrop-shaped Italian tomatoes)
- 16 pitted black olives
- 16 sun-dried tomatoes, thinly sliced
- 4 tablespoons chopped fresh dill
- 4 teaspoons Dijon mustard
  Juice of 2 limes
- 1 cup extra-virgin olive oil
  Boston lettuce
  Fresh dill sprigs for garnish

Prepare fire for grill. Season tuna with salt and white pepper and grill until medium, about 2 minutes per side. Let tuna cool and cut into strips.

Mix chopped vegetables, olives, sun-dried tomatoes, dill, mustard, lime juice and olive oil in large bowl. Season with salt and white pepper. Add tuna strips and let marinate a few minutes to pick up the flavors.

Arrange a bed of Boston lettuce on chilled plates, mound vegetables on lettuce and arrange tuna strips across top. Garnish each with a sprig of dill.

Serves 2 as entrees, 4 to 6 as a side salad.

Beef Tenderloin on a Bed of Sweet Onions With Creole Mustard Sauce

- 6 ounces beef tenderloin per person
  Creole Cravings meat seasoning to taste
- 2 tablespoons clarified butter
- 3 sweet onions (such as Texas 1015s), thinly sliced
  Salt and pepper if needed
  Creole Mustard Sauce (recipe follows)

Season beef with meat seasoning and lightly rub with clarified butter. Broil to desired doneness. Slice when ready to serve. Saute onions until soft and slightly caramelized; place on serving plate or platter. Arrange beef on top. Serve with Creole Mustard Sauce.

Creole Mustard Sauce

- ¼ cup finely diced carrot
- ¼ cup finely diced onion
- 1 teaspoon finely chopped garlic
- 1 tablespoon butter
- 2 cups heavy (whipping) cream
- 2 tablespoons Creole mustard
- 2 tablespoons Worcestershire sauce
  Salt and pepper if needed

Place carrot, onion, garlic and butter in a heavy saucepan and cook until vegetables "sweat," become translucent and lightly caramelized. Add cream and cook until reduced by half.

Add mustard and Worcestershire. Season to taste and add more mustard if desired. Serve with tenderloin.

Serves 4.

Creole Succotash Timbales

- 1 tablespoon vegetable oil
- ½ cup finely diced andouille sausage
- ¼ onion, finely diced (about ½ cup)
- ½ bell pepper, finely diced (about ½ cup)
- 1 ear fresh corn, cut off cob
- ½ cup lima beans
- ½ teaspoon minced fresh thyme
- ½ teaspoon minced garlic
- ½ tomato, cut in medium dice (about ½ cup)
- 3 cups heavy (whipping) cream
- 6 eggs
- Salt and ground black pepper if needed

In oil, cook andouille, then add onion and pepper, corn, lima beans, thyme and garlic. Cook until vegetables are a little soft and begin to sweat. Add tomato and cream and heat until mixture just starts to simmer. Remove from heat and add a little of the egg, whisk a few seconds, then add remaining eggs.

Butter individual 6-ounce timbale molds or a 1½-quart timbale mold or casserole (or spray with non-stick spray).

Ladle in custard mixture to fill three-fourths full. Place pan in water bath (larger pan filled with hot water to come up about 1 inch on sides of mold or casserole).

Bake slowly at 225 degrees about 1 hour or until timbale tests done when a knife inserted in the center comes out clean. Run a knife around sides and unmold.

Serves 8.

Brennan's Mile High Mud Pie

Chocolate Nut Brownie Crust
Ice Cream Filling
Cooked Meringue
Warm Chocolate Sauce

Chocolate Nut Brownie Crust
- 4 ounces unsweetened baking chocolate
- 3 ounces (6 tablespoons) butter
- 5 ounces sugar (about 1 cup)
- 2 eggs, beaten
- 3 ounces (1 cup less 2 tablespoons) all-purpose flour
- 3 ounces chopped pecans

Melt chocolate and butter in the top of a double boiler (or microwave on medium-50 percent power 3 to 5 minutes; stir to smooth). In mixing bowl, combine melted chocolate with sugar, 2 beaten eggs, flour and pecans; mix well.

Spread in well-greased 9-inch aluminum foil or other pie pan. Bake at 350 degrees until crisp). Cool and refrigerate.

Ice Cream Filling
- ¾ cup chocolate ice cream
- ¾ cup coffee ice cream
- ¾ cup vanilla ice cream

Soften ice creams and layer each flavor 2 inches thick in 1 or 1½-quart round bowl in this order: chocolate, coffee and vanilla. Freeze until very hard, at least 4 or 5 hours and preferably 8 to 10. Turn ice cream out into brownie crust. (Run warm water over bowl or place bowl in warm water for a few minutes.)

Cooked Meringue (Italian Meringue)

- 4 egg whites, stirred to blend
- 8 ounces (1 cup plus 2 tablespoons) sugar

Combine stirred egg whites and sugar in top of a double boiler over simmering water and cook to 120 degrees on a candy thermometer. Start preheating oven to 500 degrees. Remove egg white mixture from heat and whip until stiff.

Spread over ice cream completely. Put frozen dessert in preheated 500-degree oven until meringue is lightly browned. Refreeze. Serve cut in wedges with Warm Chocolate Sauce.

Warm Chocolate Sauce
- 8 ounces semisweet chocolate, broken up
- 1 cup whipping cream
- ½ ounce brandy

Combine chocolate and whipping cream in top of a double boiler over simmering water. Cook, stirring, until melted and smooth. Remove from heat and stir in brandy. Keep warm.

May also be prepared in microwave: melt chocolate in cream in a 1-quart glass batter bowl on medium (50 percent) power. Stir and add brandy. Keep warm.

Brennan's
3300 Smith St.
Houston, Texas 77006
522-9711

Cafe Adobe

FAVORITES

Cafe Adobe's Chicken Taco Salad

Cafe Adobe's Shrimp Enchiladas With Ranchero Sauce

Cafe Adobe's Mexican Pizza

Cafe Adobe's Sopabananapilla

Austin's Seafood Stuffed Mushrooms

Austin's Meatloaf

Austin's Texas Brownie Pie

Cafe Adobe is only one of the "personality" restaurants created and owned by entrepreneur Beau Theriot, whose first effort was The Brownstone.

In the early 1970s the Brownstone was known for its creative decor—tented paisley ceiling, Lalique chandelier and antique chairs and water glasses—and gourmet specialties such as avocado soup and Beef Wellington.

Theriot moved with the times and changing tastes in food; he opened Cafe Adobe in 1980, Adobe Dos (on Voss Road just south of Woodway, in 1986, the multi-tiered Oasis on Lake Travis in Austin which can serve 1,200, Austin's (in early 1988 in the original Brownstone location near River Oaks), and most recently Jose Loco in Austin.

Theriot bought a house in Acapulco about three years ago, but moved back in '88 to give the former Brownstone a redo as Austin's which now serves "casual creative country" food.

He wanted Cafe Adobe to be a casual, happy place with an atmosphere that tells guests to "relax and have a good time." He gave the remodeled adobe-colored building the exuberance of a Mexican plaza with umbrella tables, fountains, statuary, hanging baskets of ivy and other plants.

Downstairs there is a shady courtyard and several bar and dining areas. They are defined by arched doorways, dark box-beam and pierced tin ceilings, banquettes, screens and fireplaces.

A stylized multicolor flower-butterfly-bird print covers some banquettes, walls and a matching ceiling in counterpoint to other walls either painted adobe color or covered with color-coordinated prints.

Upstairs there is the Party Room and the Acapulco Bar where guests can have drinks and appetizers inside or on an outside deck with a treetop view of the skyline.

With the help of Carmen Campos, who also had been chef at The Brownstone, Theriot created his version of super-fresh, non-greasy Tex-Mex.

Among specialties are fajita nachos, a "make-your-own" combo platter, light meals, combination plates featuring chalupas and tacos al carbon, and Mexican breads and pastries.

Star Attractions

★ Casual, fun setting with a plaza-like atmosphere; courtyard and several fountains. Seats 160 inside; 150 outside.

★ Every Friday night is theme costume night for waiters; prizes are awarded for best costume.

★ Open seven days a week for lunch and dinner.

★ Private Party Room that can accommodate 150.

★ Fiesta Feast for Two with choice of eight items including chalupa, Potato Skins Mexicana, grilled chicken and sopapillas.

Cafe Adobe's Chicken Taco Salad

- 3 tablespoons margarine or oil
- 3 cloves fresh garlic, finely minced
- 1 cup chopped celery
- 1 cup chopped green bell pepper
- 1 large tomato, chopped
- 1 medium-size white onion, finely chopped
- 3 bay leaves
- 2 pounds boneless skinless chicken breasts
- 1 quart water
- Salt and pepper to taste
- 6 crispy shells made from 11-inch flour tortillas
- Shredded lettuce
- Diced tomatoes for garnish
- Grated cheese
- ¾ cup guacamole for garnish
- ¾ cup sour cream for garnish
- Sliced jalapenos (optional)

Melt margarine in a pot and saute garlic, celery, bell peppers, tomato and onion. Add bay leaves, chicken breasts and water. Salt and pepper to taste; cook covered over moderate heat 45 minutes or until chicken is tender.

When chicken is cooked, cool and cut into small pieces. Return chicken to pot and keep warm.

Fill crispy tortilla shells three-fourths full with shredded lettuce. Drain chicken and place equal parts on top of lettuce. Arrange diced tomatoes and grated cheese on top of chicken.

Garnish with 2 tablespoons each guacamole and sour cream. Sprinkle with sliced jalapenos.

Serves 6.

Cafe Adobe's Shrimp Enchiladas With Ranchero Sauce

Clean shrimp (3 large shrimp per person) and peel. Grill, basting with garlic butter (melted butter seasoned with garlic powder) and a small amount of chopped cilantro; do not overcook. Chop shrimp. Fry one corn tortilla in oil just until soft.

Mix shrimp with grated white cheese (such as queso blanco or Monterey Jack) and place on tortilla. Pour Ranchero Sauce over top, covering well. Top with more cheese and run under grill to melt.

Ranchero Sauce
- 2 cups canned stewed tomatoes
- 3 fresh jalapeno peppers (remove seeds for milder taste)
- 1 tablespoon chicken seasoned stock base or instant chicken bouillon granules
- 1 teaspoon garlic powder
- 1 teaspoon cayenne red pepper (or to taste)
- 1 cup chopped green onions
- 2 tablespoons oil

Pour stewed tomatoes into blender with the jalapenos, chicken base and garlic powder; blend well. Pour blended mixture into a medium saucepan.

Add cayenne, green onion and oil. Heat sauce to a boil and simmer 15 minutes, stirring occasionally. Cover enchilada with sauce. Makes 2 cups sauce, enough for 10 to 12 enchiladas.

Cafe Adobe's Mexican Pizza

Fry a 10-inch flour tortilla until light brown. Spread lightly with refried beans.

For beef pizza: lightly spread cooked ground beef, Ranchero sauce and Jack cheese over tortilla.

For chicken pizza: lightly spread shredded cooked chicken, Ranchero sauce and Jack cheese over tortilla.

For supreme pizza: lightly sprinkle chopped onion, bell peppers, mushrooms, cooked beef or chicken (or both). Top with Ranchero sauce and grated Jack cheese.

Put pizza in 350-degree or microwave oven to melt cheese. Top each pizza with a spoon of guacamole and arrange a circle of jalapenos around guacamole.

Each serves 1.

Sopabananapilla

Cafe Adobe's rich version of sopapillas, fried Mexican pastries.

> **Vanilla Pudding (recipe follows)**
> **Sopapillas (recipe follows)**
> 1 banana, sliced
> **Whipped cream and ground cinnamon for garnish**

Prepare pudding and sopapillas. To serve: Place sopapilla on plate; top with pudding and sliced banana. Garnish with whipped cream and a sprinkle of cinnamon.

Serves 2.

Vanilla Pudding
- ⅓ cup sugar
- 1 tablespoon cornstarch
- ⅛ teaspoon salt
- 2 cups milk
- 2 egg yolks, slightly beaten
- 2 tablespoons butter, softened
- 2 teaspoons vanilla

Blend sugar, cornstarch and salt in 2-quart saucepan. Whisk milk and egg yolks together; gradually stir into sugar mixture. Cook over medium heat, stirring constantly with a wire whip until mixture thickens and boils.

Boil and stir 1 minute. Remove from heat; stir in butter and vanilla and continue stirring until smooth. Cool slightly, then chill in refrigerator. Use in Sopabanapilla or serve as pudding.

Sopapillas
- 1 cup all-purpose flour
- 1 tablespoon shortening
- 1 teaspoon baking powder
- Dash of salt
- Hot water

Mix flour, shortening and baking powder. Add enough hot water to form a dough. Divide into one-inch balls.

Sprinkle flour on counter or table and roll each ball of dough into a 4-inch circle. Heat oil to 350 degrees in deep fat fryer. Add sopapillas.

With a spoon, sprinkle hot oil over sopapillas while they are cooking so they will rise. When puffed up, remove from deep fat fryer with a slotted spoon. Drain on paper towels.

Austin's Seafood Stuffed Mushrooms

1½	cups butter
3	cloves garlic, crushed
1	cup finely chopped white onion
½	ounce Cognac
½	cup finely chopped chives
1	pound cooked shrimp, chopped
1	pound fresh lump crabmeat
1	cup finely chopped celery
1	cup finely minced parsley
⅓	teaspoon rosemary
1	tablespoon Parmesan cheese
1	cup bread crumbs
1	tablespoon Worcestershire sauce
	Salt and white pepper
48	medium-size mushroom caps

Melt ½ cup butter in skillet. Saute garlic and onions; add Cognac and simmer 1½ minutes. Add chives, shrimp, crab, celery, parsley, rosemary, Parmesan, bread crumbs and Worcestershire sauce.

Season with salt and white pepper. Mix well. Stuff mushroom caps and place in a buttered ovenproof dish. Pour 1 cup melted butter over stuffed mushrooms and bake at 350 degrees 35 minutes.

Serves at least 12.

Austin's Meatloaf

1	pound lean ground beef
	Salt and pepper to taste
1	medium onion, chopped
1	medium bell pepper, chopped
½	cup finely chopped celery
2	eggs
2	tablespoons milk
2	tablespoons Meatloaf Sauce (recipe follows)

Salt and pepper meat. Mix onion, bell pepper and celery and combine with meat. Add eggs, milk and 2 tablespoons meatloaf sauce; mix well. Form into a loaf and place in 9x5x3-inch loaf pan.

Bake uncovered at 350 degrees until done, about 35 minutes. Serve with remaining Meatloaf Sauce.

Serves 3 to 4.

Meatloaf Sauce

½	cup brown sugar
½	cup ketchup
⅓	cup soy sauce

In small saucepan, mix brown sugar, ketchup and soy sauce. Simmer on low heat 5 minutes.

Austin's Texas Brownie Pie

½	cup all-purpose flour
¾	cup sugar
⅓	cup butter
4	ounces baking chocolate
2	eggs
½	teaspoon vanilla extract
½	cup semisweet chocolate chips
½	cup chopped pecans
1	unbaked deep dish 10-inch pie shell

Preheat oven to 350 degrees. Sift flour and sugar in a medium bowl.

In a small pan, melt butter and baking chocolate (or melt chocolate in microwave on 50 percent power; stir to smooth). Do not let it get too hot or it will become grainy.

Whisk chocolate into flour mixture. Add eggs and mix very well. Add vanilla extract, chocolate chips and chopped pecans.

Fit pastry into pan. Pour mixture into pie shell and bake at 350 degrees 45 minutes. Serve warm with vanilla ice cream or fresh whipped cream.

Serves 6 to 8.

Austin's
2736 Virginia
Houston, Texas 77098
520-5666

Cafe Adobe
2111 Westheimer
Houston, Texas 77098
528-1468

Cavatore Italian Restaurant

> ### FAVORITES
>
> *Spinaci con Mozzarella*
> Spinach With Mozzarella Cheese)
> *Fettucini Pescatore*
> (Fettucini With Seafood)
> *Pollo Arrosto al Rosmarino*
> (Breast of Chicken With Rosemary)
> *Vitello con Scallops Bianchina*
> (Veal and Sea Scallops Bianchina)
> *Melanzane Parmigiana*
> (Eggplant Parmesan With Marinara Sauce)
> *Cafe Cavatore*

The design of Cavatore's emblem, a blend of American, Texas and Italian flags and a stylized Lone Star, sets the theme for this rustic restaurant, which is equal parts of Italy and Texas with a generous dash of provincial whimsy.

The emblem appears in stained glass windows, on waiters' aprons, matchbook covers and unique matchbook notepads (a memento for non-smokers).

The restaurant extends a big Texas welcome with traditional Italian specialties in the informal setting of a 100-year-old barn. The owners found the barn in Bastrop and thought it would make a natural companion to their other restaurant, La Tour d'Argent, housed in an old log cabin (see page 52)

They moved the barn to a site just across the street from La Tour on Ella Boulevard just off Loop 610. Then they painstakingly repaired and rebuilt it as close to the original as possible with wooden floors and walls and sheet metal ceiling. At one point to get enough sheet metal to preserve the ceiling's authenticity, partner Sonny Lahham said he even advertised in the newspaper for rusty sheet metal.

By advertising in a newspaper in Milan, Italy, where partner Giancarlo Cavatore's mother still lives, they found a treasure trove of memorabilia to line the walls.

Old movie posters (originals of Fellini's "8½" and Sophia Loren movies), banners from Italy's '84 world soccer championship, vintage newspapers (including World War I front pages), photographs and family mementos help to create the unique decor.

Another bit of whimsy is the cover of the laminated menu, which is a colorful cartoon map of Columbus sailing toward America with a boat load of foodstuffs. Photos of historic figures, family, friends and even family pets are worked into the scene.

Add to the setting the happy sounds of live piano music and the cheerful buzz of clinking glasses, conversation and laughter in the dining rooms, bar and new outside deck and you can expect a fun dining experience.

The food goes beyond spaghetti and meatballs despite the casual red-and-white-check tablecloth decor. Among specialties are traditional pastas—Fettucini Carbonara and Alfredo—seafood, a variety of veal and chicken preparations and desserts such as cannoli and spumone.

At lunch, the restaurant fills with the business crowd from Galleria, downtown, the nearby Heights, Northwest Mall and River Oaks. At dinner, guests are an eclectic mix.

Star Attractions

★ Setting—"The oldest barn in Houston" with a fascinating array of memorabilia, stained glass windows, baskets, fresh flowers and plants.

★ Outside deck with umbrella tables.

★ Small garden where fresh herbs and a few vegetables are grown, perhaps the eggplant you're having as Eggplant Parmesan for dinner.

★ Live piano music every night except Sundays.

★ Tableside food preparation; two specials daily are prepared at the table.

★ Wine list with more than 100 selections; good choices from Italy (especially the fine wines of the Piedmont area), France and California.

★ Accommodations for private party.

★ Dessert tray.

★ For non-smokers, souvenir matchbook-size note pads.

Fettucini Pescatore
(Fettucini With Seafood)

- 2 pounds fresh fettucini
- 12 shrimp, cleaned and peeled
- 12 mussels, cleaned
- 16 sea scallops
- 1 tablespoon chopped garlic
- 1 tablespoon chopped capers
- ½ cup heavy (whipping) cream
- ¼ cup clarified butter
- Salt and pepper

Cook fettucini and drain. Saute shrimp, mussels and scallops in large saute pan with garlic. Add capers and cream and simmer over low heat 5 minutes.

Mix with fettucini and serve immediately. Garnish as desired.

Serves 4.

Spinaci con Mozzarella
(Spinach With Mozzarella Cheese)

- ½ pound fresh spinach, washed and trimmed
- 1 tablespoon extra-virgin olive oil
- 1 clove garlic, sliced
- Salt and pepper to taste
- 1 ounce Mozzarella cheese

Drop spinach in boiling water for about 5 minutes, then remove and drain well.

In saute pan, heat oil and saute spinach with garlic. Add salt and pepper to taste. Put spinach in a ramekin or small individual casserole, top with Mozzarella and bake at 350 degrees until cheese melts.

Note: Can cook spinach in microwave covered with only the water clinging to the leaves. Drain well. Proceed as directed in recipe, but microwave casseroles on medium high power until cheese melts.

Serves 2.

Melanzane Parmigiana
(Eggplant Parmesan)

    Salt and pepper
18 (¼-inch thick) slices peeled eggplant
3 eggs, beaten
    Flour
1 quart Marinara Sauce
16 slices very thin Mozzarella

Salt and pepper eggplant slices and dip into beaten eggs, then dip lightly into flour. Deep-fry in a skillet in a small amount of oil. Set them aside as they are cooked, drain on paper towels and keep warm.

Place a layer of Marinara Sauce on the bottom of a deep baking tray or rectangular casserole. Cover with a layer of eggplant slices, stacked two deep, on top. Pour Marinara Sauce over all and top with slices of Mozzarella. Bake at 350 degrees 5 minutes, or until cheese melts.

Serves 6.

Pollo Arrosto al Rosmarino
(Breast of Chicken With Rosemary)

4 (8-ounce) chicken breasts
    Flour
    Clarified butter
½ pound fresh mushrooms, cleaned and sliced
2 garlic cloves, chopped
    Fresh rosemary
1 cup brown sauce (make from scratch, canned or made from mix)
2 ounces brandy

Lightly flour chicken breasts and saute in a little clarified butter 10 minutes. Discard fat.

Saute mushrooms and garlic in a few tablespoons butter and add fresh rosemary and chicken. Let saute a few minutes, then add brown sauce and let cook over high heat 3 minutes. Add brandy.

Serves 4.

Marinara Sauce

¼ cup extra-virgin olive oil
4 tablespoons chopped onion
4 tablespoons chopped garlic
3 tablespoons chopped fresh basil
2 tablespoons chopped fresh parsley
5 cups peeled, fresh tomatoes, pureed (can use canned)
    Salt and pepper to taste

Heat oil in saucepan over medium heat. Add onion, garlic, basil and parsley; simmer a few minutes. Add pureed tomatoes and simmer 1 hour.

Add salt and pepper to taste. Makes 1 quart.

Vitello con Scallops Bianchina
(Veal and Sea Scallops Bianchina)

- ¾ pound veal scallopini
- 6 ounces sea scallops
- Flour
- 1 tablespoon clarified butter
- ½ cup dry white wine
- Few teaspoons (¼ ounce) fresh lemon juice
- ½ cup veal or chicken stock
- Salt and pepper

Lightly flour veal and scallops. Heat butter in skillet and saute veal 8 minutes until done, but still moist; season with salt and pepper. Deglaze pan with wine, lemon juice and stock (simmer, scraping up any browned bits from bottom). Let stock cook to reduce about 5 minutes.

Serves 2.

Cafe Cavatore
(Cavatore Special Coffee)

- 1 ounce hazelnut liqueur
- 1 ounce orange liqueur
- 1 cup brewed coffee
- 1 ounce freshly whipped cream
- ¼ ounce coffee liqueur

Mix hazelnut and orange liqueurs in a coffee cup and fill with hot coffee. Top with whipped cream and coffee liqueur.

Makes 1 cup.

Cavatore Italian Restaurant
2120 Ella Blvd.
Houston, Texas 77008
869-6622

DeVille

FAVORITES

Smoked Lamb Nachos With Poached Tortilla Chips, Refried Black Beans and Pico de Gallo

Campfire Salmon

Charcoaled Axis Venison With Red Bell Pepper Sauce

Low-Cal Green Apple and Jicama Slaw

Seven Grain Bread

Cobbler of Peaches, Basil and Cherries With Southern Comfort Sauce

---

The last few years have seen the renaissance of grand hotel food, and one of the trendsetters on the local scene is The Four Seasons Hotel-Houston Center.

Since the hotel opened in 1982, it has been identified with fine food and food events including an annual tasting of Bordeaux wines, Italian festival, movie Oscar Awards party, civic, fine arts and charity benefits, and fine food in the context of a health-promoting alternative menu of calorie- and fat-controlled meals. The hotel has been host to top chefs from the U.S. and Europe for the Evening of the Masters benefit for Cystic Fibrosis.

In 1984, the Four Seasons co-sponsored the first Festival of Southwest Cookery which cast an early spotlight on the chefs, leaders and foodstuffs of this important trend of the 1980s.

The current keeper of the Four Seasons culinary flame is executive chef Robert McGrath, 34, a Kentucky native who is making a national reputation for contemporary Southwestern food. A graduate of the Culinary Institute of America in Hyde Park, N.Y., and a gold medal-winning chef, he was on the American Culinary Federation's U.S. Culinary team in 1986.

In June, 1988, Food & Wine magazine named him one of America's Ten Best New Chefs in the magazine's first annual awards. In September, 1988, he was one of 12 American-born chefs (two from Texas) named as finalists in the first American Culinary Gold Cup Bocuse D'Or national cooking event.

All the hallmark ingredients of regional Texas and Southwestern cooking appear on McGrath's menu—Gulf Coast shrimp, oysters, crab, quail, venison and other game, salsas, cilantro, flour tortillas and blue corn tortilla chips.

DeVille, the hotel's showcase restaurant, overlooks the new George R. Brown Convention Center. The sophisticated restaurant attracts executive travelers, business and social movers and shakers as well as Houston diners with a culinary curiosity about Southwestern cuisine.

They come for such signature dishes as Big Spring rattlesnake with toasted pumpkin seeds on ancho linguini with a lime cream or quail breast wrapped in veal bacon (produced in-house) on black pepper cream.

For a bit of fun McGrath created a dessert called Holy Cow Empanadas: marzipan, part tinted with cocoa to produce a mottled "cowhide" pattern, and filled with espresso-soaked ladyfingers and mascarpone cheese, served with a chocolate Chartreuse liqueur sauce.

Star Attractions

★ Creative contemporary cuisine with the emphasis on fresh ingredients and Southwestern specialties by one of the nation's up-and-coming chefs.

★ Almost all specialties including smoked meats and fish are prepared on the premises—a wide variety of breads, sausages, pates, smoked bacon, salamis, hams, smoked salmon, custom desserts, pastries and ice creams. Some herbs are being grown in a small roof garden.

★ Sunday brunch which includes a large selection of a-la-carte entrees plus appetizer bar, salad buffet and desserts.

★ Catering (in-house or off-site)—from small parties to events for thousands.

★ Delivery to nearby offices ($25 service fee for fewer than 15 people.)

★ Hotel offers various dining facilities including lobby lounge featuring live entertainment, Terrace Cafe and 24-hour room service for guests.

★ Frequent host to celebrities. You might catch a glimpse of anyone from Luciano Pavarotti to Sting.

★ Subdued elegance, comfortable and quiet enough for pleasant conversation while dining.

★ Dine poolside through room service or pool cafe. Year-round swim club memberships available. Call the public relations department for information.

★ Convenient to the downtown performing arts theaters—The Wortham Center, Jones Hall and Plaza, Alley Theater and Music Hall. Have dinner before or after the theater and avail yourself of complimentary courtesy car service in the downtown area.

★ Philosophy of supporting Houston civic and fine arts groups and contributing food for the hungry through the Food Loop program of the End Hunger Network.

Smoked Lamb Nachos

½ pound smoked lamb tenderloin
8 ounces poached tortilla chips
6 tablespoons refried black beans (recipe follows)
6 tablespoons pico de gallo (recipe follows)

Prepare lamb and accompaniments. To serve: Arrange beans, tortilla chips, sliced lamb and pico de gallo in vertical strips on a plate. Garnish with a cilantro sprig.

Serves 4.

Smoked Lamb Tenderloin
Season tenderloin with salt and pepper and grill (using mesquite wood) according to personal preference. Tenderloin also can be cooked in a smoker or cast iron skillet or can be broiled. Keep covered until ready to use, then slice and arrange on plate.

Poached Tortilla Chips

½ teaspoon finely chopped garlic
1 teaspoon finely chopped jalapeno
6 ounces corn tortilla chips
3 ounces heavy (whipping) cream
1½ ounces grated Monterey Jack cheese

In a hot skillet place garlic and jalapeno and cook, covered, until they begin to "sweat." Quickly add tortilla chips and cream; simmer until reduced by half. Top with the grated cheese. Keep warm.

Diet Alert: Use lighter cream or half-and-half and part-skim Monterey Jack cheese.

Refried Black Beans

1 pound black turtle beans
  Water
1 head garlic (8 to 10 cloves), coarsely chopped
2 quarts chicken stock
½ jalapeno, finely chopped
½ small onion, diced

Soak the beans in water 8 to 10 hours. Drain in a colander. Place beans, enough water to cover, garlic, stock, jalapeno and onion in a large pot and boil 20 minutes; then reduce heat and simmer slowly 2 to 3 hours, adding a little water occasionally if necessay.

Use leftover beans in burritos. Roll beans into salami shapes and saute in hot butter in skillet until reheated. Place on warm flour tortillas, roll up and serve with sour cream and pico de gallo.

Pico de Gallo

- 3 large tomatoes, diced (about 3 cups)
- 1 onion, chopped (1 cup)
- 3 to 4 cloves garlic, minced
- 1 small fresh jalapeno, finely chopped
- 1 small bunch cilantro, chopped (1 cup)
- Juice of 3 limes (½ cup)
- ½ medium jicama, peeled and chopped (1 cup)

Combine diced tomatoes, chopped onion, garlic, jalapeno, cilantro, lime juice and jicama. Drain if necessary because mixture should be crunchy, not soupy.

Note: For best texture, hand-chop all ingredients. It helps to use firm pink tomatoes and seed them before dicing.

Makes about 6 cups.

Campfire Salmon With Braised Fennel

- 4 (6- to 7-ounce) salmon fillets (not steaks)
- 2 large fennel bulbs, julienned
- 1 teaspoon chopped garlic
- 1 bunch fresh chives, chopped
- 1 quart chicken stock
- 1 tablespoon hickory smoke powder
- 4 each "turned" carrots, zucchini and yellow squash, cooked (see Note)

Prepare grill or smoke box and place the salmon fillets on the grill. Cook over a moderately high flame 4 minutes; reduce heat to moderately low and grill covered 10 to 12 minutes.

In a hot skillet, add the fennel and quickly stir in the garlic. Move the skillet continuously over the heat 2 to 3 minutes. Add the chives, then the chicken stock. Boil until reduced to half.

Place the fennel-chicken stock mixture on the plate in the center. Place the salmon off-center on the braised fennel. Garnish with carrot, zucchini and yellow squash.

Note: Turned vegetables are small pieces of vegetables hand-carved in football shapes with seven sides. Use carrots or squash about 1-inch in diameter and cut in uniform 2-inch pieces. Cut each piece in halves or quarters.

Hold each piece in one hand between thumb and index finger and trim in a rounded arc while gradually turning piece with fingers. Pieces should be thicker in the middle and tapered to pointed ovals.

For vegetables like zucchini and squash, leave one side showing some color. Use a thin, sharp paring knife with a 2½ or 3-inch blade. At some gourmet housewares shops, you may find special tourne knives with curved blades.

Charcoaled Axis Venison With Grilled Summer Vegetables and Red Bell Pepper Sauce

2 (2½- to 3-ounce) venison medallions per person
Herb Marinade (optional)
Olive Oil just to cover meat

Herb Marinade: Combine a few tablespoons fresh chopped parsley with crushed thyme, rosemary, sage, garlic and basil to taste. Mix with oil and pour over meat. If time permits, marinate covered two days.

Before charcoaling, wipe off excess oil. The remaining oil will cook off, so you end up with a nice flavoring from the herbs with no added calories.

Red Bell Pepper Sauce
- 2 tablespoons light oil
- 1 clove garlic, chopped
- 4 shallots, chopped
- 4 red bell peppers, seeded, stemmed and cubed
- 6 tablespoons white wine
- 1 cup chicken stock
- ½ teaspoon cayenne pepper or less to taste
- ½ teaspoon ground cumin (cominos)
- Salt and freshly ground black pepper

Heat oil and saute garlic and shallots 1 minute in skillet over low heat.

Add cubed peppers and saute 5 minutes until peppers begin to soften, but don't allow garlic and shallots to brown.

Add white wine and chicken stock and bring to a boil. Season with cayenne pepper, cumin, salt and black pepper. Simmer until peppers are soft.

Transfer mixture to a food processor or blender and puree until smooth. Return to saucepan and simmer until puree is reduced to the proper consistency. Spoon onto plate and top with meat.

The cayenne makes this a very nippy sauce; it is also delicious with other grilled meats or chicken.

Low-Cal Green Apple and Jicama Slaw

- 1 large or 2 small red bell peppers
- 3 medium-size tart green apples
- 1 medium-size jicama
- 1 tablespoon chopped fresh parsley
- 3 tablespoons tarragon vinegar
- 6 tablespoons rice vinegar
- 3 tablespoons honey (preferably Texas Marigold), optional
- Salt and freshly ground white pepper

Roast, peel and seed red pepper and cut into julienne strips. Peel, core and cut apples into matchstick-size pieces. Peel and cut jicama into matchsticks.

Combine red pepper, apple, jicama, parsley, vinegars, honey, salt and white pepper. Toss until well mixed. Serve cold and crispy.

Serves 6 to 8.

Cobbler of Peaches, Basil and Cherries With Southern Comfort Sauce

This is Robert McGrath's contemporary version of cobbler and involves a unique crust and assembly. The dough is delicious, but very delicate. It must be thoroughly chilled before rolling. If it becomes too soft at any time, return it to the refrigerator and chill until firm again.

At DeVille, the cobbler is served in individual tart shells. Half of the dough is used for the bottom crust(s).

Half the remaining dough is rolled out and baked on a cookie sheet, then crumbled and mixed in with the fruit filling. The remaining raw dough is rolled out (it may be necessary to chill it again), cut into strips and arranged lattice-fashion over the filling, then baked.

It is easier at home to make it as a two-crust cobbler in one large tart pan as described below or to make it open face, still mixing some of the baked strips into the filling.

¾	pound cold butter
¾	cup sugar
5	teaspoons grated lemon rind
1½	teaspoons honey
1	cup yellow cornmeal
1½	cups all-purpose flour
1	teaspoon salt
3	egg yolks
1½	teaspoons vanilla

Cut cold butter into chunks and cream with sugar a few minutes in heavy duty mixer, adding lemon rind and honey.

Blend cornmeal, flour and salt. Add to mixer bowl and beat a minute or two. Add egg yolks and vanilla and beat until smooth, scraping down sides of bowl once or twice (mixture should remain pretty cold).

Turn dough out onto large sheet of plastic wrap and divide in half. Fold wrap over each and press or roll out into two rounds. Refrigerate until thoroughly chilled, 4 hours or even overnight.

When ready to use, roll each into a ¼-inch thick round, sprinkling with masa harina (Mexican corn flour) or flour to prevent sticking. Using cardboard circles as guides, cut one round to fit bottom of a 9-inch tart pan with removable bottom. Cut another round 10 inches in diameter. Slide smaller pastry round off cardboard into pan.

Spoon filling over dough, leaving a ¾-inch border around edge. Place top crust over filling and let sit a few minutes until dough softens enough to sink down into pan slightly.

With the heel of your hand, press down around scalloped edge of pan to trim excess dough. Discard trimmings or re-roll.

Cut vent holes. Bake at 350 degrees 10 minutes, reduce heat to 300 or 325 and continue baking about 40 minutes or until golden brown.

Variation: Roll dough out, cut bottom crust and place in pan. Chill. Roll half of remaining dough ¼-inch thick on cookie sheet and bake at 350 degrees until golden brown, 20 minutes or longer. Cut into strips. Let cool, crumble and mix with fruit.

Meanwhile, cut one long strip of dough and press along sides or use scraps of dough and press into place around sides.

Cut remaining unbaked dough into strips and arrange lattice-fashion over top. Bake at 350 degrees 10 minutes. Reduce heat to 300 degrees and bake until golden brown.

Peach and Cherry Filling

2	pounds seeded, unpeeled ripe peaches
12	ounces pitted black cherries or dried sour cherries
1	leaf fresh basil, torn
1	tablespoon fresh lemon juice
1	tablespoon sugar
2	tablespoons masa harina (Mexican corn flour)

Cut peaches into 1-inch wedges or bite-size pieces. Toss with cherries and basil in lemon juice. Sprinkle sugar and the masa harina on top and distribute evenly. Fill tart shells as directed.

Southern Comfort Sauce

1 quart half-and-half
1 vanilla bean, split
7 egg yolks
¾ to 1 scant cup sugar
⅓ cup Southern Comfort

Scald the half-and-half with the vanilla bean (heat until bubbles form at edges). Meanwhile, beat the yolks and sugar to a ribbon. Strain the milk and remove vanilla bean.

Pour a little of the egg yolks into the warm milk, then add the egg mixture to the milk, whisking briskly, until sauce will form a ribbon stream when dropped from the end of a spoon.

Pour the entire mixture into a clean pot and heat over low heat and cook, stirring constantly, until sauce will coat the back of a spoon. Remove and place pan over ice until cool. Whisk in the Southern Comfort with a wire whip. Refrigerate.

Seven Grain Bread

1¼ cups Seven Grain Cereal
1½ teaspoons salt
3 tablespoons unsulphured molasses
1 tablespoon sugar
2 cups hot water
½ cup extra-virgin olive oil
2 packets (½ ounce) active dry yeast
1 cup warm water (110 degrees)
1½ cups whole-wheat flour
1½ cups rye flour
1 pound (4 cups) unbleached all-purpose flour

Combine cereal, salt, molasses, sugar, hot water and oil in a large bowl and let soak 1 hour.

Dissolve yeast in 1 cup warm water and combine gradually with cereal mixture, whole-wheat, rye and all-purpose flours on low speed of electric mixer. Mix to moisten and let stand 10 minutes.

Knead until dough is elastic and cleans sides of bowl, adding more flour if necessary.

Place in a draft-free spot and let rise until almost tripled in bulk. Punch dough down and knead briefly.

Shape into baguette loaves and place on lightly greased cookie sheet or jellyroll pan. Let rise again until increased about one-third. Bake at 350 degrees 45 minutes to 1 hour.

Makes 2 loaves about 3½ inches wide and 14 inches long.

DeVille
Four Seasons Hotel-Houston Center
1300 Lamar
Houston, Texas 77010
650-1300

Empress of China

FAVORITES

*Empress Avocado Shrimp
with Tangy and Spicy Sauce*

Karbar Beef Strings

Sesame Scallops

Sand on the Snow

Empress Peking Roasted Chicken

Broccoli in Special Garlic Sauce

Empress of China executive chef Scott Chen and manager Richard Ho have developed a new concept of Chinese cooking which they have christened Nouvelle Chinese Cuisine. They don't go along with the philosophy that just because Chinese cuisine has been good or 2,655 years it can't be changed or improved.

Chen incorporates ideas, ingredients and traditional cooking techniques from many different cuisines to achieve a unique style. The food is Chinese; the presentation, French.

The decor of the 95-seat restaurant also is non-traditional. The contemporary feeling is created by neutral colors punctuated by burgundy table linens, cane back chairs and planter boxes filled with fresh flowers. The distinctive blue and white china was special-ordered from Taiwan.

Instead of resorting to the expected and often trite stir-frys, Chen employs a repertoire of cooking techniques that result in lighter, healthier dishes—steaming, poaching, boiling, braising, sauteing, grilling and broiling, or a combination.

Wok "firing" and broth cooking replace frying. In wok firing, the combination of heating the oil to a very high temperature and using a lighter breading prevents retention of grease. In broth cooking, no fat is used; foods are cooked in broth, then flambeed in spices.

Likewise, Richard Ho does not feel bound by tradition in matching wines to the dishes, and makes gifted pairings with the Chinese food from an extensive list ranging from French Pouilly Fuisse to California Cabernet. He lists more than 50 fine Bordeaux alone.

Although the nouvelle dishes are lower in calories, sodium and cholesterol, they don't taste like wimpy diet fare, and portions are ample. The emphasis is on accentuating the natural flavors of the fish, seafood, poultry and vegetables. No monosodium glutamate flavor enhancer is used, and low-sodium soy sauce and Maggi seasoning are often substituted for soy sauce.

Classics are modified to reduce fat; sweet and sour pork, for example, is made with 98 percent fat-free pork.

Empress of China is recommended by Pritikin and Weight Watchers in the North Harris County area. Still, the No. 1 consideration is good taste. Skillful cooking, seasoning and presentation elevate the food to gourmet status, and the restaurant also has received accolades from gourmet societies and corporations that have entertained there.

Chen's family immigrated to Houston from Taiwan in 1981 and he became interested in cooking while working at The Ambassador, a Chinese restaurant owned by his sister-in-law. While working at Uncle Tai's restaurant he learned the classic Hunan-style cooking. Travels have broadened his appreciation of many cuisines.

Richard Ho was born in Hong Kong but grew up in Lubbock, Texas, where he earned bachelor's and master's degrees at Texas Technological University. He also has a master's degree in business administration from the University of Houston.

Ho, his wife Vicky and Chen are the three major stockholders in the restaurant corporation.

Star Attractions

★ Nouvelle Chinese cuisine, innovative lighter, healthier cooking style that emphasizes good taste and incorporates the best tastes and cooking techniques of many cuisines.

Specialties include Oriental beef or chicken "fajitas" and several dishes with fanciful names—Sand on the Snow (chicken flambeed with black pepper and a wine sauce), the Clash of the Titans (prawns, chicken and beef sauteed with vegetables), Neptune's Platter (sea scallops, shrimp and crab with black bean sauce) and Romeo and Juliet (scallops in a spicy ginger sauce for two).

★ Special attention is paid to freshness of ingredients, innovative combination of herbs and seasonings and sauces that enhance rather than smother. All natural ingredients are used; no artificial flavors or preservatives. Because each dish is prepared to order, spiciness or ingredient selections can be adjusted to the guest's taste.

★ Open kitchen policy during operating hours. Guests may visit kitchen on request.

★ Daily specials—both food and wine.

★ Extensive wine list with about 300 selections including 50 fine Bordeaux. Excellent price-to-value ratio; prices challenge those in retail shops. Two or three new wines are featured every week; currently any wine featured as a weekly special is $12 a bottle.

★ Moderately priced Sunday brunch buffet of 15 courses.

★ Gourmet wine dinners and party menus. Six to 10-course special banquet available for groups of more than seven.

★ Cooking classes including supermarket shopping trip.

★ Registered dietitian serves as menu consultant.

★ Delivery within a 10-minute drive of the restaurant.

★ All menu items available for take-out.

Avocado Shrimp With Tangy and Spicy Sauce

½	pound medium-size shrimp, cleaned and peeled
2	avocados
1	teaspoon Chinese horseradish mustard
3	teaspoons sugar
1	teaspoon extra-virgin olive oil
2	teaspoons vinegar
3	teaspoons fresh lemon juice

Halve the avocados lengthwise; discard seeds.

Bring enough water to cover shrimp to a boil in a pot. Add shrimp, cover and set aside off heat until shrimp are pink, 2 to 5 minutes. Drain and cool shrimp under cold running water 2 to 3 minutes.

Combine horseradish mustard, sugar, oil, vinegar and lemon juice; mix well. Mix cooled shrimp and spice mixture.

Fill avocado with shrimp and pour leftover sauce on top. Serve cold.

At Empress of China, this is served as an appetizer. The avocado is thinly sliced, lined up on the plate in overlapping slices and topped with a row of shrimp and sauce.

Karbar Beef Strings

At Empress of China, these are precooked in the kitchen and finished at the table on small hibachis.

- 1 pound beef flank steak
- ¼ cup soy sauce
- ¼ cup bottled oyster sauce
- 2 teaspoons sesame oil
- 1 garlic clove, crushed
- 1 teaspoon each minced fresh ginger, fresh lemon juice and Chinese chili sauce (Sriracha is one brand)

Cut beef into ½-inch strips with the grain, holding knife at a 45-degree angle. Add mixture of soy sauce, oyster sauce, oil, garlic, ginger, lemon juice and chili sauce to taste. Mix well and marinate at room temperature 1 hour. Cover and refrigerate overnight.

Remove beef strips and thread onto skewer.

Preheat broiler and place rack 3 to 4 inches from heat. Broil beef strips until done, about 2 to 4 minutes. Serve with Chinese barbecue sauce, available in cans in Chinese markets.

Serves 4.

Broccoli in Special Garlic Sauce

- 1 pound broccoli florets
- 2 teaspoons chopped scallions
- 1 teaspoon chopped fresh ginger root
- ½ teaspoon chopped garlic
- 1 teaspoon hot chili paste (canned Szechuan chili sauce)
- 1 teaspoon wine or sherry
- ½ teaspoon salt
- 1 teaspoon sugar
- 1 teaspoon rice wine vinegar
- 4 teaspoons water
- ½ teaspoon cornstarch

Bring a small amount of water to a boil in a saucepan. Cut broccoli into bite-size pieces, drop into boiling water and parboil 2 minutes. (Or cook in a tablespoon or two of water in microwave on high.) Remove and drain.

Run cold water over broccoli 2 to 3 minutes. Arrange broccoli on a clean plate.

Mix scallions, ginger root, garlic and hot chili paste. Mix wine, salt, sugar, vinegar, water and cornstarch well.

Heat wok and add 2 teaspoons sunflower oil. Stir-fry until scallion-ginger mixture imparts its fragrance.

Add wine mixture, bring to a boil and pour over broccoli.

Serves 4 to 6.

Sesame Scallops

- ¾ pound large sea scallops, cleaned
- 1 cup peanut oil
- 1 teaspoon fresh lemon juice
- 1 teaspoon white wine
-   Cornstarch
- ½ cup cornmeal
- 2 teaspoons sesame oil
- 1 tablespoon fresh garlic, peeled and minced
- ¼ teaspoon sesame seed
- 1 teaspoon fresh minced ginger
- 2 teaspoons soy sauce
- 1 teaspoon bottled oyster sauce
- ¼ hot Chinese chili sauce
- ½ teaspoon rice vinegar
- 4 teaspoons chicken stock
- 1 teaspoon wine
- ½ teaspoon sugar

Heat wok and add 1 cup peanut oil. Pat scallops dry. Add lemon juice and wine. Toss scallops in cornstarch, then in the cornmeal until each scallop is finely coated.

When oil is medium hot and bubbling, add coated scallops carefully one by one and wok-fry them to light golden brown, about 2 minutes. Remove scallops and set aside to drain.

Wipe the wok clean and reheat. Heat 2 teaspoons sesame oil in wok and stir-fry garlic, sesame seeds and minced ginger.

Pour in combined soy sauce, oyster sauce, chili hot sauce, rice vinegar, chicken stock, wine and sugar.

Dissolve 2 teaspoons cornstarch in 1 tablespoon water; mix well. Add cornstarch mixture and cooked scallops to wok and stir-fry 5 to 10 seconds until coated. Remove from pan, arrange on plates and serve.

Sand on the Snow

⅔	pound boneless, skinless chicken breast.
	Salt
	Water
1	egg white
	Cornstarch
½	cup sunflower oil
¼	teaspoon baking soda
½	pound broccoli florets
½	teaspoon wine or sherry
1	teaspoon sugar
¼	teaspoon black pepper
1	cup chicken stock or water
1	garlic clove, peeled andd mashed

Slice chicken in thin slices, add ¼ teaspoon salt, 1 tablespoon water and lightly beaten egg white. Mix well.

Add 1 teaspoon cornstarch, mix and let stand 20 minutes.

Bring 2 quarts water to a boil to cook broccoli.

Heat wok and add oil. When oil is medium-hot, bubbling, put chicken in wok and stir-fry until it turns white.

Remove chicken and drain off oil. The used oil may be used again for precooking other dishes.

Add ¼ teaspoon baking soda to boiling water. Add broccoli. When water returns to the boil, about 30 seconds, remove broccoli and arrange around the rim of a plate.

Mix wine, ½ teaspoon salt, 1 teaspoon sugar, ¼ teaspoon black pepper, 1 cup chicken stock and ½ teaspoon cornstarch.

Clean the wok and heat it. Put 1 teaspoon sunflower oil in wok and stir-fry garlic. Add wine-stock mixture and bring to a boil. Add chicken. Mix well, cook lightly, remove from pan and arrange on top of broccoli.

Empress Peking Roasted Chicken

One of the most popular specialties on the Empress of China menu, this is the restaurant's interpretation of Peking duck.

1	(3-pound) chicken
1	teaspoon salt
½	cup soy sauce
¼	teaspoon Chinese five-spice powder
3	teaspoons bottled oyster sauce
1	teaspoon honey
2	teaspoons fresh ground ginger
1	teaspoon sherry or white wine
1	garlic clove, peeled and minced
½	cup plum sauce (duck sauce—can use bottled)

Clean chicken and sprinkle inside and out with salt. Combine soy sauce, five-spice powder, oyster sauce, honey, ginger, sherry and garlic in a large container. Toss chicken in marinade until coated inside and out. Let sit at room temperature 1 hour.

Cover and refrigerate overnight. When ready to cook, preheat oven to 350 degrees. Remove chicken from marinade and pat dry with cloth.

Put chicken on rack in roasting pan and roast 20 minutes at 350 degrees. Turn chicken and roast it 20 more minutes. Increase oven temperature to 450 degrees. Turn chicken and roast it 15 minutes. Turn, and roast 15 more minutes, 1 hour 10 minutes cooking time in all.

To serve, cut chicken into small pieces and serve with plum sauce on the side.

Serves 4.

Empress of China
5419A FM 1960 West
Champions Village III
Houston, Texas 77069
583-8021

Hunan River

> ### FAVORITES
>
> *Four Delight of Kung Pao*
> *Imperial Two Flavors*
> *Steamed Scallops and Vegetables*
> *Broccoli in Garlic Sauce*
> *Red Pepper's Dry Sauteed String Beans*
> *Red Pepper's Shrimp Fried Rice*

Hunan River is changing its address but not its style, "fine Chinese country cooking." Still in River Oaks Shopping Center on West Gray, it is moving up in the neighborhood to a free-standing building only a block or so west of its old location and should be relocated in time to celebrate the next Chinese New Year.

The restaurant's more spacious new home is contemporary in design with a patio garden setting with fountains. Owners Wen and Shirley Lee also own the Red Pepper at 5626 Westheimer. It opened in July, 1987, with virtually the same menu as Hunan River.

Wen Lee, who was born in mainland China, grew up in Taiwan and finished college there. He came to the U.S. in 1964 for graduate courses at the University of Connecticut, then worked for an insurance company in New York before moving to Houston in 1976 and becoming a restaurateur.

The Lees say that fine Chinese cooking requires the perfect combination of taste, smell and color, and they believe the natural flavors of the food should determine the taste of each dish. They use no MSG (monosodium glutamate flavor enhancer) or frozen ingredients in their regular dishes and buy only fresh, fine quality seafood, meat and vegetables, said Wen Lee.

The menu also features steamed diet dishes that have no artificial ingredients or seasoning.

The Lees consider their menus merely suggestions. Hunan cuisine is usually thought of as hot and spicy (hot items are printed in red on the menu), but spiciness can be adjusted to taste because each dish is cooked to order. They are happy to switch meat, poultry or fish in the sauce or add a vegetable or two to create a unique dish.

Lunch is served seven days a week, and Hunan River caters to business patrons with a special luncheon menu. The restaurant also is open until 1 a.m. on weekends with the full menu to accommodate after-theater and other late-night diners.

Hunan River was among the first Houston restaurants offering home delivery.

Among special dishes are hot appetizers including steamed dumplings and Hunan-style entrees such as General Tso's Chicken, Orange Beef, Shredded Pork With Bean Curd and Scallion in Hot Black Bean Sauce.

For those who like things on the milder side there are such dishes as Zechung Duck, sliced duck with snow peas and broccoli in a mild spiced ginger sauce; Mongolian Beef with green onion; fried rice and soft noodle dishes.

Ordinarily desserts are not an important component of Chinese menus, but at Hunan River you'll even find almond cheesecake and pecan pie with ice cream. They share space on the list with the more traditional Honey Bananas, Wok Fried Pudding and lychee nuts.

Chinese recipes look lengthy, but are not difficult because most of the ingredients are seasonings. To make these dishes you will need to stock your pantry with such Chinese ingredients as whole small dried red peppers, Szechuan hot pepper sauce, winter pickle, canned ginger water, dried shrimp, sesame oil and rice wine vinegar. They are available at most Oriental markets (see Shopping Guide), and some can be made at home.

Because some ingredients are salty, taste and add salt only if needed. You can often substitute chicken broth for some or all of the oil and use low-sodium soy sauce to cut calories and sodium.

Spellings vary depending on regional dialects so you may find the same product under several different names.

Star Attractions

★ Fine Chinese country cooking with a wide variety of menu items representing various regional cooking styles. Spiciness adjusted to taste.

★ Open seven days a week with convenient hours for lunch and late night dining from the full menu. Open until 11 p.m. weekdays and to 1 a.m. Fridays and Saturdays.

★ Healthful light dishes; no artificial ingredients or seasoning.

★ Home delivery and take-out.

★ Catering.

★ Special bar drinks.

Four Delight of Kung Pao

Kung Pao means any kind of meat or seafood sauteed with whole small dried peppers and roasted peanuts in a hot spicy sauce.

- 4 ounces raw boneless chicken
- 4 ounces diagonally sliced beef such as flank steak
- 4 jumbo shrimp, peeled and butterflied
- 4 large sea scallops
- 1 tablespoon oyster sauce
- 1 egg, lightly beaten
- 1 tablespoon cornstarch
- 1 tablespoon salad oil
- 6 (2-inch) whole dried red peppers
- 1 scallion, chopped in ¼-inch pieces
- 2 garlic cloves, peeled and minced
- 1 ounce fresh ginger root, minced
- ⅓ cup roasted peanuts
- Vegetable oil
- Sesame oil
- Sauce (recipe follows)

Combine chicken, beef, shrimp and scallops. Combine in order listed, to make a marinade: oyster sauce, egg, cornstarch and salad oil, stirring thoroughly after adding each.

Heat 4 cups oil in wok; quickly stir-fry meat and seafood. When all is partially cooked, drain oil and set food aside.

Heat 1 tablespoon fresh oil in empty wok. Add the dried pepper, scallion, garlic and ginger. Stir-cook 10 seconds until flavor develops. Add meats, seafood and peanuts and quickly stir-fry another 10 seconds. Add sauce and stir-fry 10 seconds. Turn off heat and splash a little sesame oil over the food. Stir and serve immediately.

Sauce

- 6 tablespoons soy sauce (Kikkoman recommended)
- 2 tablespoons chicken or meat broth
- 1 tablespoon white wine
- 1 teaspoon vinegar
- 1 tablespoon sugar
- 1 teaspoon hot pepper sauce (Szechuan spicy sauce)
- ¼ teaspoon ground black pepper
- 1 tablespoon cornstarch
- ½ teaspoon sesame oil

Whisk together soy sauce, broth, wine, vinegar, sugar, pepper sauce, black pepper, cornstarch and oil. Use as directed.

Steamed Scallops and Vegetables

This is a low-calorie, low-fat dish from Hunan River's menu of diet dishes.

- ½ pound sea scallops
- 1 teaspoon baking soda
- 6 to 8 each: snow peas, chopped broccoli florets, baby corn, water chestnuts, straw mushrooms (or fresh) and chopped Chinese cabbage
- 4 tablespoons hoisin sauce
- 4 tablespoons soy sauce

Put baking soda in a large bowl filled with cold water and clean sea scallops by swishing around in the water. Drain soda water, then rinse scallops in cold water about 20 seconds.

Mix scallops with vegetables and put in steamer (preferably a bamboo steamer).

Put 1 inch of water in a wok and set steamer over water (be sure it doesn't touch water). Simmer 20 minutes. Add warm water to the wok if water level gets too low.

Serve the food in the steamer with hoisin sauce and soy sauce on the side.

Diet Alert: use low-sodium soy sauce.

Imperial Two Flavors

- 6 ounces beef tenderloin, cut in 1-inch cubes
- 6 jumbo shrimp, peeled and butterflied
- 1 teaspoon garlic salt
- 1 egg, slightly beaten
- 1 tablespoon cornstarch
- 1 tablespoon salad oil
-   Vegetable oil
- 1 green bell pepper, cut in 1-inch pieces
- 1 scallion, cut in ¼-inch pieces
- 1 (1-ounce) piece fresh ginger, minced
- 2 garlic cloves, peeled and minced
- 10 fresh snow peas with both ends cut off
-   Sauce (recipe follows)
- ½ teaspoon sesame oil

To the beef and shrimp, add the following in order listed, stirring well after each: garlic salt, beaten egg, cornstarch and salad oil.

Heat 4 cups oil in a wok and add beef and shrimp mixture and green pepper. Quickly stir-fry until slightly cooked. Drain oil and set food aside.

Heat 1 tablespoon fresh oil in empty wok. Add scallion, ginger and garlic and stir-fry 10 seconds until flavor develops. Return beef, shrimp and green pepper to wok. Add snow peas and quickly stir-fry 10 seconds.

Add sauce and stir-fry 10 seconds. Turn off heat and splash ½ teaspoon sesame oil over the food. Stir briefly to mix. Serve immediately.

Sauce

- 4 tablespoons soy sauce
- 2 tablespoons chicken or meat broth
- 1 tablespoon wine
- 1 tablespoon vinegar
- 1 tablespoon sugar
- ½ teaspoon ground flower pepper seeds (available at Chinese food stores)
- 1 tablespoon bottled oyster sauce
- 1 teaspoon hot pepper sauce
- 1 tablespoon cornstarch

Combine all ingredients. Stir sauce just before using so sugar and cornstarch are thoroughly dissolved.

Makes 1 platter.

Red Pepper's Shrimp Fried Rice

-   Oil
- 6 ounces fresh baby shrimp
- 4 tablespoons finely chopped onion
- 2 eggs, scrambled
- 4 cups steamed rice (cold steamed short grain rice is best)
- 3 tablespoons chicken broth
- 2 tablespoons soy sauce
- 1 tablespoon oyster sauce
- ½ teaspoon ground black pepper
- 1 teaspoon sesame oil

Heat 2 tablespoons oil in wok. Add shrimp and onion and stir-fry 10 to 15 seconds. Remove from wok and set aside.

Heat 2 more tablespoons oil in wok, add scrambled eggs and stir quickly 5 seconds. Remove wok from heat (don't let eggs overcook). Add rice and stir with egg until evenly mixed. Return wok to heat and add shrimp and onion, broth, soy sauce, oyster sauce and pepper; continue stir-frying 20 seconds.

Splash sesame oil over top and stir another 5 to 10 seconds. Serve immediately.

Small pieces of meat, seafood or vegetables may be used instead of shrimp.

Serves 2 or 3.

Broccoli in Garlic Sauce

1 (1-pound) bunch broccoli
Vegetable oil
10 water chestnuts, chopped
⅓ cup ("a handful") dried black mushrooms, cut in small pieces and soaked in warm water 1 hour
4 garlic cloves, peeled and minced
1 ounce fresh ginger root, minced
1 scallion, cut in ¼-inch pieces
Sauce (recipe follows)

Cut stems off broccoli and separate heads into florets (use stems in another dish, or discard). Heat 4 cups oil in a wok. Add broccoli and fry 10 to 15 seconds, until it is partially cooked. Drain oil and let broccoli drain on paper towels.

Heat 1 tablespoon fresh oil in the empty wok. Add garlic, ginger and scallion and stir-fry 10 seconds. Add water chestnuts, soaked mushrooms and broccoli and stir-fry another 10 seconds.

Add sauce and continue stirring 10 to 15 seconds.

Turn heat off and splash ½ teaspoon sesame oil over broccoli. Stir briefly and serve immediately.

Sauce
4 tablespoons soy sauce
1 tablespoon ginger water (see Note)
1 tablespoon white wine
1 tablespoon vinegar
2 tablespoons sugar
¼ teaspoon ground black pepper
1 teaspoon Szechuan hot pepper sauce
1 tablespoon cornstarch

Combine ingredients in order listed, stirring well between each addition.

Note: Ginger water is available in cans in Oriental markets. To make it at home, cut one piece of fresh ginger root in chunks and cook in 1 cup boiling water about 30 minutes. Don't let water boil away.

Red Pepper's Dry Sauteed String Beans

Vegetable oil
1 pound green string beans, cut in 2-inch pieces
3 ounces ground pork (optional)
1 tablespoon Chinese winter pickle (see Note)
1 tablespoon minced dried shrimp (optional)
1 teaspoon minced fresh ginger
2 tablespoons chopped scallion
3 tablespoons chicken or meat broth
1 tablespoon soy sauce (use sparingly as winter pickle and dried shrimp are salty)
1 teaspoon sugar
1 tablespoon white wine
¼ teaspoon black pepper
1 teaspoon sesame oil

Heat 4 cups oil in a wok. Add beans and fry 20 to 30 seconds. Drain oil and set beans aside.

Heat 1 tablespoon fresh oil in the empty wok. Add ground pork and stir-fry until well done. Return beans to wok and add winter pickle, shrimp, ginger, scallion, broth, soy sauce, sugar, wine and pepper. Stir-fry 20 to 30 seconds. Splash sesame oil over top and continue stirring 5 to 10 seconds. Serve immediately.

Red Pepper
5626 Westheimer
Houston, Texas 77056
622-7800

Hunan River
W. Gray – River Oaks Shopping Center
Houston, Texas 77019
527-0200

Kim Son

> ### FAVORITES
>
> *Spring Rolls (Goi Cuon)*
> *Salted Crabs With Black Pepper*
> *(Cua Rang Muoi)*
> *Charcoal Broiled Beef With Lemon Grass*
> *(Bo Nuong Xa)*
> *Vietnamese French Coffee*

The success of Kim Son is a story of family determination, hard work and dream fulfillment. In Vinh Long, a village in Vietnam, Kim Tran had a restaurant for 20 years, but when the Communists took over in Vietnam she and her husband Son La, their five sons and one daughter fled their homeland in a boat. They lived 14 months as refugees in Indonesia, then immigrated to Houston in 1980.

Kim worked for a Vietnamese restaurant for a year, and she and the family saved their money. In 1982, they opened Kim Son, which means Golden Mountain (the name also stands for the family names—Kim for the mother, and Son for the father). It is managed by their son Tri Minh La. In July, 1986, they opened the second Kim Son on Wilcrest; it is run by another son, Tan La, and Kim's sister, Anh, is cook.

Other Vietnamese refugees to Houston who had known the restaurant in Vinh Long helped make Kim Son an almost instant success. But Houston was ready for the spicy-hot Vietnamese food, a natural extension of Tex-Mex and Hunan Chinese, and the restaurant quickly became popular with anyone who appreciates good food and "Mom's cooking"—Vietnamese style.

The original Kim Son, just east of downtown near the George R. Brown Convention Center, seats about 200 in a boxy unpretentious building. It is often filled to capacity, especially on weekends, and diners are almost equally divided between those who use chopsticks and regular cutlery.

The menu features 236 items; more than half are typical of South Vietnam, whose hot, humid climate resembles Houston's. Chinese food also is well represented on the menu because there are strong ties between Vietnamese and Chinese food; Chinese is the banquet and special occasion food of Vietnam.

Many of the Vietnamese-Chinese ingredients are similar—rice, bok choy and other greens, cilantro, bean sprouts, peppers and ginger root. But Kim Son also offers Houston diners the opportunity to become familiar with such exotic tastes as lemon grass (citronella root), sticky (sweet or glutinous rice, also traditional in Thai cooking), Nuoc Mam, the ubiquitous bottled fish sauce which is Vietnam's salt and pepper, and dried lily buds.

Waiters will recommend dishes and explain eating etiquette on request for those unfamiliar with Vietnamese food (it especially takes practice to develop the art of eating the black pepper crabs with chop sticks as neatly as the Vietnamese and Chinese diners). Hands-down favorites are spring rolls, Vietnamese egg rolls and charcoal broiled beef with lemon grass.

For "beginners" or those who prefer milder food, a suggested menu is Hot and Sour Soup, spring rolls, two or three entrees (for four people) including fish, chicken, beef and/or pork or a combination plate), rice and French coffee with condensed milk. A good accompaniment is beer—Chinese (Tsing Tao) or Japanese (Kirin)—jasmine tea or fresh lemonade.

Both spring rolls and egg rolls have rice paper wrappers, but spring rolls are larger and are not deep fried. The spring roll filling is a mixture of shrimp, pork, vegetables and vermicelli. Spring rolls are served with a vegetable platter containing lettuce, mint leaves, cilantro and a peanut sauce.

The smaller, crisper egg rolls are filled with chopped meat, green onion and vermicelli. To eat, you roll each up in a lettuce leaf and dip the end in the accompanying fish sauce.

Fresh fruit is usually the dessert of choice, but Kim Son also features traditional desserts made with red bean jelly and coconut milk as well as lychees, longans and flan cake, which resembles Mexican flan or French creme caramel.

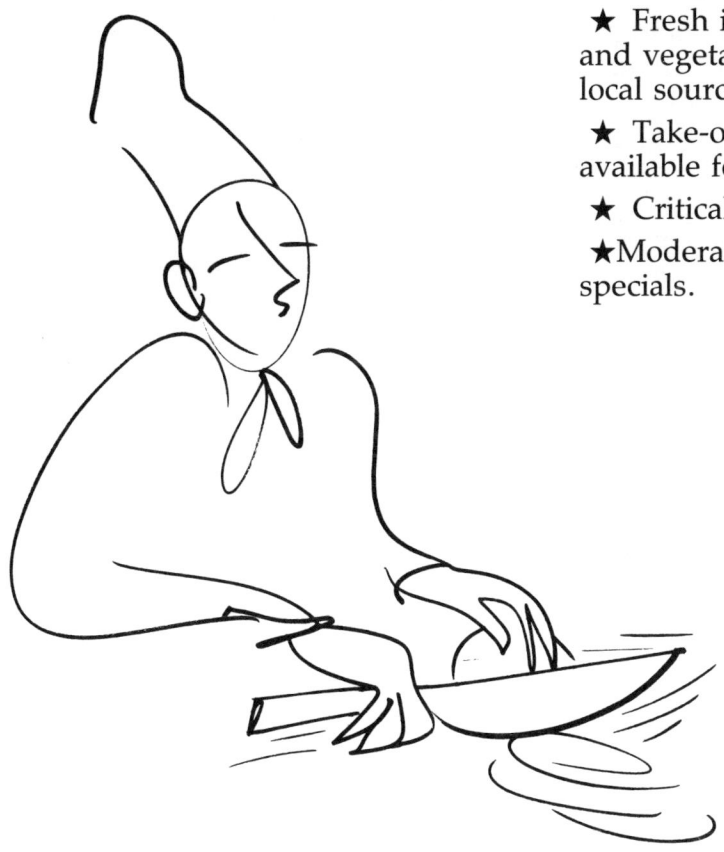

Star Attractions

★ Open seven days a week with extended hours—at the St. Emanuel location, 8:30 a.m. to midnight daily through Sunday and to 3 a.m. on Fridays and Saturdays; at Wilcrest, hours are 10:30 a.m. to 11 p.m. daily.

★ Traditional Vietnamese breakfast served all day. It features Pork Congee rice soup (weekends only), steamed rice cakes with various fillings and sticky rice dishes.

★ Vietnamese a la carte specialties such as shrimp on sugar cane, House Special Soup (a delicious combination of meat and seafood with mixed vegetables and tamarind in a clear dark broth), stir-fried chicken with hot chilies and lemon grass, House Special Seafood and a variety of noodle dishes including special vermicelli. Chinese specialties include won ton soup, Kung Pao Chicken and stir-fry dishes.

★ Special menus for parties, weddings and receptions.

★ Banquets for groups from 10 to 250.

★ Fresh ingredients—many, such as herbs and vegetables, are obtained directly from local sources.

★ Take-out. Almost all menu items are available for take-out.

★ Critical acclaim from restaurant reviewers.

★Moderate prices; inexpensive daily lunch specials.

Kim Son's Spring Rolls

16	shrimp (16- to 20-count per pound), cleaned, cooked and shelled (see note).
1	pound lean boneless pork such as tenderloin, trimmed of fat, cooked (see note)
1	cup hoisin sauce
1	cup chicken broth
½	cup creamy peanut butter
2	tablespoons sugar
2	tablespoons cornstarch dissolved in cool water
2	to 4 tablespoons chopped peanuts
16	round pieces rice paper (12 inches in diameter)
1	portion (1 coil) vermicelli (thin, string-like rice noodles), cooked, drained and cut into 1-inch lengths
¼	pound fresh bean sprouts
1	pound (1 medium head) leaf lettuce, separated into leaves
	Fresh mint leaves

Note: To cook shrimp, drop into boiling seasoned water to cover; turn heat off, cover pan and let sit about 5 minutes until pink. Drain and rinse with cold water. Peel and cut shrimp in half lengthwise.

To cook pork, place in pot with water almost to cover and bring to a boil, cover pan, reduce heat and simmer until done. Remove from pan, cool and cut pork into 3x1x⅛-inch slices.

Combine hoisin sauce, chicken broth, peanut butter and sugar in a saucepan and cook, stirring, over medium heat until well blended and sugar is dissolved. Whisk in the dissolved cornstarch and stir over low heat until smooth and sauce is somewhat thickened. Add a few tablespoons chopped peanuts.

Dip each rice paper in lukewarm water and let soften about 30 seconds to 1 minute. Straighten the rice paper out on table or counter.

Put half a lettuce leaf at lower part of rice paper. Top with a few of the vermicelli pieces, bean sprouts and 1 to 2 pieces of mint.

Fold two sides of rice paper toward the center into a rectangle about 4 inches long, then roll up like a cylinder adding 2 or 3 slices of pork and 2 shrimp halves as you roll. At Kim Son they also add a couple of sprigs of green onion which extend from one end of the cylinder. To serve, dip into peanut sauce.

Serves 8

Salted Crabs With Black Pepper

This traditional dish is probably the most popular item on Kim Son's menu. The crab can be served as an appetizer (the Vietnamese like to have them with wine or beer while sitting around and talking to their friends), or the crab can be served as an entree with rice. They are messy to eat, but fans of this dish say it's definitely worth the effort.

2	pounds large hard-shell crabs (2 or 3 per person)
1	cup chopped onion
¼	pound butter
2	tablespoons sugar
2	tablespoons bottled oyster sauce
¼	teaspoon salt
	Freshly ground black pepper

Clean crabs in cold water. Twist and remove the skirt attached to the underside. Remove spongy parts attached to the interior. Pull away top shell. Wash and dry the crabs and chop each in half.

Deep-fry in oil heated to 450 degrees until crab turns red.

Heat wok over high heat. Combine onion, butter, sugar, oyster sauce and salt in wok, and heat until butter melts. Add the crab and stir-fry about 5 minutes. Sprinkle generously with pepper and serve immediately on a platter.

To eat: break them apart with nut crackers and suck meat out of the claws.

Charcoal Broiled Beef With Lemon Grass

1	pound lean beef (such as flank steak), cut in 2-inch wide pieces
1	tablespoon sugar
1	tablespoon honey
	Salt to taste
1	tablespoon crushed lemon grass
1	tablespoon crushed garlic
1	tablespoon soy sauce
¾	teaspoon cornstarch
1	tablespoon oil
	Rice papers (6 inches in diameter)
	Lettuce
	Fresh mint leaves
	Bean sprouts, sliced cucumber, sliced carrot and plantain (about 2 tablespoons per person and 4 plantain slices)

Place beef in a bowl. Add sugar, honey, dash of salt, lemon grass, garlic, soy sauce, cornstarch and oil. Marinate in refrigerator overnight. Grill over charcoal until done to taste.

To serve—Soften rice paper by dipping in bowl of lukewarm water. Place a small piece of lettuce, mint leaves, bean sprouts, carrot and plantain in the rice paper and the beef on top. Roll up in a cylinder shape.

To eat, dip in fish sauce (nuoc mam) made by mixing 3 cups bottled nuoc mam and 1 cup vinegar.

Serves 3 to 4.

Vietnamese French Coffee

2	tablespoons coffee (Cafe du Monde preferred)
	Canned sweetened condensed milk

Note: This is made in a special coffee cup with filter, available at Vietnamese markets. Place coffee in coffee filter and screw in place. Spoon 2 tablespoons condensed milk in cup and place filter on top. Fill the filter with hot water and let it drip through. Stir to combine with condensed milk, then pour over ice in a glass.

If you like hot coffee, just add more hot water.

Serves 1.

Kim Son
8200 Wilcrest at Beechnut
Houston, Texas 77072
498-7841

Kim Son
1801 St. Emanuel at Jefferson
Houston, Texas 77003
222-2461

La Reserve

FAVORITES

Chilled Artichoke Soup
Spring Salad With Boursin Wontons
Poached Flounder With Peppercorn Cream Sauce
Chicken With Green Asparagus Coulis
Medallions of Lamb With Three Mushrooms and Basil Sauce
Lemon Tart

La Reserve, the showcase restaurant at the Inn on the Park hotel, provides the ultimate pleasurable dining experience for the gourmet, the romanticist or the status-minded.

The hotel dominates a 28-acre park-like setting where black swans glide over a reflecting pond. Thousands of cars may be humming along one of Houston's busiest freeways just beyond the trees, but the Palm Court with its waterfall fountains and greenery is an oasis of serenity.

The atmosphere in La Reserve also is calm, but not stuffy. A recent multimillion dollar renovation has changed the look but not the elegant ambiance; there are tasteful touches of beveled glass, black lacquer and rich coordinated floral, stripe and solid fabrics in soothing greens, coral and rose.

The restaurant is now centered by Le Pavilion, a glassed-in dining area with draped crystal chandelier and mirrored ceiling which is perfect for private parties.

Inn on the Park has been one of Houston's favorite settings for weddings, receptions, gourmet wine dinners and other special occasions since it opened in 1981.

The hotel is Houston's only American Automobile Association Five-Diamond Award winner. The hotel and La Reserve both rate four stars from Mobil, and the restaurant has received the Travel Holiday Award four consecutive years.

Currently presiding over the kitchen is executive chef Kaspar Donier, who began his apprenticeship at 16 in Zurich. French cooking remains one of his fortes, but he has an innate talent for matching classic French techniques to Texas regional cuisine and the best and freshest local ingredients.

Among recent successes are a mousse of Texas pheasant with blueberry vinaigrette, fried chicken salad with sweet onions and herb cheese biscuits and scallopini of wild boar with grapes and green pepper sauce.

The sophisticated diner, especially one who enjoys wild game, will luxuriate in the adventurous fare—from sauteed Axis deer medallions with peaches and brandy to an alternative menu dinner that tastes far richer than its 500-calories.

Star Attractions

★ Degustation "Grand Menu," a fixed price six-course sampling of the chef's finest offerings.

★ Chef's specials change daily.

★ Alternative cuisine—A special menu of chef's specialties for those who wish to monitor their intake of calories, cholesterol and sodium. An appetizer and main course total less than 500 calories at lunch and 650 for dinner. The menu includes many dishes that guests order because they are delicious, not just because they are watching calories.

★ Series of vintner dinners matching vintage, and sometimes exclusive, wines to the cuisine. Call the hotel to get on the mailing list.

★ Black Swan, a unique English-style pub with live entertainment. Offers more than 75 international beers; complimentary hors d'oeuvre from 5 to 7 p.m.

★ Wonderful cakes and pastries from award-winning pastry chef Regis Bernard, one of the city's most accomplished pastry chefs.

★ Complimentary hand-dipped chocolates and cookies served after dinner.

★ Wine by the glass and a selection of champagne drinks such as Kir Royale made with apricot, plum and other liqueurs. Separate list of Cognac, Armagnac and brandies and fruit-flavored after-dinner drinks.

★ A separate dessert menu featuring Inn on the Park's signature souffles, Hot Apple Tart with Cinnamon Ice Cream and Cookie Basket with Assortment of Sorbets and Strawberry Sauce.

★ Lavish Sunday brunch in Cafe on the Green.

★ Buffet on the Bayou—Southwestern specialties with a Cajun flair every Friday night at Cafe on the Green.

★ A perfect ending to a night on the town or a romantic getaway weekend—the Viennese Dessert Table, a breathtaking array of cakes, flans, tarts and French pastries, Fridays and Saturdays from 10 p.m. to 1 a.m.

★ Contribute to the Food Loop program of the End Hunger Network.

Chilled Artichoke Soup

- 2 artichokes (can use hearts only)
- 1 (8-ounce) potato, peeled
- ½ (3-ounce) onion
- 2 tablespoons olive oil
- 1 quart chicken stock
- 1 bay leaf
- 1 sprig fresh thyme
- Dash of salt and pepper
- 1 cup half-and-half
- 12 chives (for garnish)

If using fresh-cooked artichokes, remove hearts from outer leaves. Cut up potato, artichoke and onion in big pieces. Sear onion in olive oil and add the artichokes, potato, chicken stock, bay leaf, thyme and salt and pepper. Let simmer 25 minutes. Season to taste with salt and pepper. Let cool.

Remove bay leaf and thyme from soup. Blend soup in blender until smooth. Add the half-and-half and season to taste. Chill soup in refrigerator for several hours. Garnish with finely sliced chives.

Serves 4.

Spring Salad With Boursin Wontons

- 1 medium zucchini (3½ ounces)
- 2 tomatoes
- ½ fresh fennel bulb (3½ ounces)
- 1 medium carrot (3½ ounces)
- ½ red bell pepper
- 4 ounces fresh mushrooms
- 1 Belgian endive (3 ounces)

Cut all the vegetables in julienne strips.

Marinade
- ¼ cup olive oil
- ⅛ cup red wine vinegar
- ½ teaspoon coarse grain mustard
- Dash of salt and pepper
- ½ teaspoon honey
- 1 sprig fresh basil

Combine oil, vinegar, mustard, salt, pepper, honey and basil in a bowl; mix well. Add the vegetables and marinate several hours in the refrigerator.

Wontons
- 12 wonton wrappers
- 2 ounces Boursin cheese (half a cheese)
- ¼ bunch spinach, blanched and chopped
- 6 chives

In the middle of each wonton, place a little Boursin, spinach and chives. Seal edges of the wonton and deep-fry.

Place marinated vegetable salad in center of a chilled plate and arrange the hot wontons around it.

Serves 4.

Poached Flounder With Peppercorn Cream Sauce

- 4 (5-ounce) flounder fillets
- 1 cup dry white wine
- 1 shallot (¾ ounce)
- 1 garlic clove
- 1 sprig fresh thyme
- ½ teaspoon crushed black peppercorn
- 1 cup heavy (whipping) cream
- Dash of salt and pepper

Combine wine, shallot, garlic and thyme in large frying pan. Bring to a simmer and add 2 fillets. Place lid on pan to steam the fish about 4 to 6 minutes, until milky white.

With a wide spatula, remove fillets from pan and keep warm. Repeat process with remaining fillets. If liquid starts to evaporate, add a little water. Remove steamed fillets from pan and keep warm.

Add the peppercorns and cream to pan. Let mixture cook until reduced to desired consistency. Season to taste with salt and pepper.

Place fillets on plates and pour sauce on top. Serve with a green vegetable and rice.

Serves 4.

Diet Alert: Substitute lighter cream, half-and-half or milk for heavy cream or use part cream, part chicken broth.

Chicken With Green Asparagus Coulis

- 4 (6-ounce) chicken breast halves
- Dash of seasoning mix (salt, pepper, paprika and nutmeg)
- ¼ cup olive oil
- 1 pound fresh green asparagus
- 1 garlic clove, chopped
- 1 shallot, chopped
- 1 ounce (2 tablespoons) butter
- 1 cup chicken stock

Season chicken breasts with seasoning mix. Pan-fry the breasts in olive oil until golden brown.

Cut 2 inches off top and 1 inch off bottom of the asparagus. Discard the bottom part. Cook the asparagus tips in a small amount of salted water about 4 minutes, then immediately plunge into cold water to stop cooking and preserve color. The tips will be used as garnish on the plate.

Saute the garlic and shallot in butter and add the middle part of the asparagus. Add chicken stock and simmer, covered, about 5 minutes. Process well in blender. Season to taste.

Pour the asparagus puree on bottom of plate and place chicken breast on top. Garnish with the warm asparagus tips and chopped fresh dill.

Serves 4.

Medallions of Lamb With Three Mushrooms and Basil Sauce

- 8 (3-ounce) lamb medallions, cut from the loin
- Dash of salt and pepper
- ¼ cup olive oil
- 1 shallot, chopped
- 6 fresh mushrooms, sliced
- 12 shiitake mushrooms (2 ounces), sliced
- 1 package enoki mushrooms, sliced
- 1 cup dry white wine
- 1 cup chicken stock
- ½ cup heavy (whipping) cream
- 1 sprig fresh basil, chopped

Season the lamb medallions with salt and pepper. Heat large skillet, add olive oil, heat and saute lamb on both sides until brown, about 5 minutes, on high heat. Remove from pan and keep warm.

In the same pan add the chopped shallot and mushrooms and saute them a few minutes. Deglaze the pan with white wine and chicken stock (cook, stirring up browned bits in bottom of pan). Let reduce by half.

Add the cream and let simmer until reduced to the desired consistency. Add basil and season to taste.

Place medallions on four plates and pour sauce on top. Garnish with a basil leaf.

Serves 4.

Lemon Tart

Sugar Dough Pie Crust
- 6 ounces butter (¾ stick), softened
- Scant 3 cups powdered sugar (13 ounces)
- 2 eggs
- 1 pound bread flour

In mixing bowl, beat butter; add powdered sugar gradually until creamy. Add the eggs, one at a time, beating until smooth.

Slowly add the flour until mixture has a paste consistency. Chill dough in refrigerator at least 4 hours.

Roll out dough between sheets of wax paper and fit pastry into a 9-inch pie plate, fluting edge. Cover dough with wax paper and place uncooked rice on top of paper to keep the crust from bubbling when baking. Bake in 400-degree oven 15 to 20 minutes. When done, remove wax paper and rice.

Lemon Cream
- ½ cup fresh lemon juice
- 5 eggs
- ¾ cup sugar
- 4 ounces (½ cup) melted butter

In top of a double boiler, blend lemon juice, eggs, sugar and butter. Cook over simmering water until the mixture thickens. Remove from heat and pour into the cooked, cooled crust. Refrigerate at least 2 hours.

Serve surrounded by raspberry sauce (puree and lightly sweeten raspberries) and garnish with a dollop of whipped cream, 2 to 3 fresh raspberries and a mint leaf.

La Reserve
Inn on the Park
Four Riverway
Houston, Texas 77056
871-8181

La Tour d'Argent

FAVORITES

Gratin de Queues de Crevettes aux Champignons Sauvages Nouilles Fraiches
(Gratin of Shrimp With Wild Mushrooms & Fresh Noodles)

Saute de Faisan aux Abricots Secs a la Creme
(Pheasant With Dried Apricots and Cream Sauce)

Medaillons de Veaux aux Endives a la Creme de Gingembre
(Veal Medallions With Endives in Ginger Cream Sauce)

Salade Frisee au Crotin de Chavignol
(Curly Endive With Goat Cheese Salad)

Asperges Sauce Mousseline
(Asparagus With Mousseline Sauce)

Flambees de Bananes Martiniquaise
(Flamed Bananas Martiniquaise)

Dining at La Tour d'Argent is a soul-satisfying and palate-pleasing experience in an unforgettable setting—a log cabin with hunting lodge decor on the wooded banks of White Oak bayou off Loop 610.

In keeping with the hunting lodge theme, the menu often features game such as buffalo, venison and elk. One of the most popular offerings is the wild game plate which combines pheasant, duck and squab. Walls are almost concealed by hunting trophies including lion and tiger skins and more than 2,000 mounted deer antlers, moose, elk and even rhinoceros heads.

The log cabin was built in 1917 and is the oldest log cabin in Houston. It was almost destroyed by fire just as it was being readied to open as a restaurant in 1981. One of the owners, Sonny Lahham, his wife and friends rented a sand blaster and scraped and renovated the burned logs one by one, and the restaurant opened only slightly behind schedule.

The romantic atmosphere is enhanced by leaded glass doors and windows, stone fireplaces, wooden tongue-in-groove floors and wood-beamed ceiling, master paintings and antiques of collector quality, fine china and flowers, usually red roses, on the tables. The 182 Queen Anne reproduction chairs upholstered in burgundy leather were hand-carved in Italy and took three years to produce, says Lahham, who is constantly on the lookout for art objects and furnishings to enhance the decor.

La Tour d'Argent is known as much for its fine French cuisine and wine cellar as its unique setting. It has earned the Mobil Travel Guide four-star award since 1984 and has been widely recognized for its cuisine and its exceptional wine list.

Executive Chef Dominique Dahmani is a classically trained French chef who has been working in kitchens since he was 10. He came to Houston from the Pyramid Room at the Fairmont Hotel in Dallas.

Star Attractions

★ French cuisine—one of the few traditional French restaurants in Houston.

★ Appealing setting and atmosphere for power lunches, business meetings, dinner to impress the boss or a date, or just to while away rainy hours over a bottle of wine with someone special.

★ Alcoves and rooms for secluded dining including the Garden Room which overlooks a gazebo, two man-made waterfalls and a small stream where ducks and geese glide by.

★ The resident wildlife—birds (including a cage of pigeons, doves and pheasant in the Crocodile Room), quail, raccoons, rabbits and squirrels provide a continuing floor show for diners.

★ Excellent and extensive wine list—particularly strong in French and California listings. The wine loft (available for small parties or tastings) stores 1,200 cases of wine. Wines dating to 1753 on display; drinkable vintages dating to 1898.

★ Polished, professional service.

★ Harpist plays for special occasions.

Saute de Faisan aux Abricots Secs a la Creme (Pheasant With Dried Apricots and Cream Sauce)

- 1 (2½-pound) pheasant, cleaned and ready to cook
- 1 cup clarified butter
- 1 each carrot and onion, sliced
- 1 tablespoon fresh thyme leaves
- 2 bay leaves
- 1 tablespoon whole black peppercorns
- 2 tablespoons tomato paste
- 2 medium tomatoes, peeled and chopped
- 2 cups dry white wine
- 2 cups brown sauce (made from the pheasant)
- 2 tablespoons chopped shallots
- 2 tablespoons sour cream
- 4 ounces dried apricots
- ½ cup heavy (whipping) cream

Make pheasant brown sauce: Heat saucepot, add butter, heat and saute carrots, onion, some of the pheasant bones, thyme, bay leaves and black peppercorns, tomato paste and chopped tomato; simmer until sauce turns brown, about 45 minutes. Remove fat from pan and add wine. Cook the brown sauce over very low heat 3 hours to reduce.

Debone pheasant. Saute in a little clarified butter 5 minutes on each side until done.

Remove pheasant from pan and discard fat. Add the shallots, ¼ cup wine, the pheasant brown sauce and sour cream and let simmer 10 minutes. Add apricots and a dash of cream. Slice pheasant and pour sauce on top. Serve with wild rice and vegetables.

Serves 2.

Gratin de Queues de Crevettes aux Champignons Sauvages Nouilles Fraiches (Gratin of Shrimp With Wild Mushrooms and Fresh Noodles)

- 1 pound jumbo shrimp, cooked and peeled
- ½ cup clarified butter
- 5 shallots, sliced
- 8 ounces fresh wild mushrooms (or regular mushrooms)
- 1 tablespoon chopped fresh parsley
- 1 cup dry white wine
- 1 quart fish stock
- 1 cup heavy (whipping) cream
- 4 ounces fresh fettucini
- 1 cup sliced or shredded swiss cheese

Heat butter in large saute pan and saute shallots, mushrooms and parsley. Add wine, fish stock and a dash of cream and let sauce reduce over very low heat 2 hours. When reduced to about ½ cup, add remaining cream and simmer 10 minutes over low heat. Meanwhile, cook fettucini.

Arrange fettucini on plate with cooked shrimp and mushrooms. Top with cheese and place in oven until cheese melts. Add the sauce and serve.

Serves 3 to 4.

Medaillons de Veaux aux Endives a la Creme de Gingembre (Veal Medallions With Endive and Ginger)

- 8 ounces veal rib eye
- ½ cup white wine
- 1 tablespoon chopped fresh ginger
- 1 Belgian endive, julienned
- Salt and pepper
- Flour
- 2 ounces (4 tablespoons) butter
- 1 cup veal stock
- ½ cup heavy (whipping) cream

Combine wine and ginger and marinate endive 24 hours. Season veal medallion with salt and pepper; dip lightly in flour on both sides. Melt butter in large saute pan and saute the veal quickly over high heat until it is brown on both sides.

Remove veal from pan and add chopped shallots, gingered wine, endive, veal stock, cream and salt and pepper to taste.

Let simmer about 10 minutes over low heat. Arrange veal on plate and serve with vegetables.

Serves 2.

Salade Frisee au Crotin de Chavignol (Curly Endive With Goat Cheese)

- 1 head curly endive
- 2 Belgian endives
- 4 ounces goat cheese rounds warmed in a hot oven a few minutes
- Dressing (recipe follows)

Cut curly endive and Belgian endive, rinse and pat dry. Warm goat cheese.

Dressing
- ½ cup red wine vinegar
- 1½ cups extra-virgin olive oil
- 1 tablespoon Dijon mustard
- 1 shallot, chopped
- Salt and pepper

Whisk vinegar with oil; add mustard, shallots and salt and pepper to taste. Toss lightly with salad greens.

Arrange salad greens on plate. Crumble goat cheese over top.

Serves 2.

Asperges Sauce Mousseline (Asparagus With Mousseline Sauce)

- ½ pound thin fresh asparagus, washed and peeled
- 1 quart boiling water
- ½ cup red wine vinegar
- 1 tablespoon cracked black pepper
- ½ cup water
- 5 egg yolks
- 1 pound clarified butter
- Juice of 1 lemon
- ½ cup whipped cream
- Salt and pepper to taste

Wash and peel asparagus if necessary. Drop into boiling salted water and cook 5 minutes. If served cold, remove from water and drop into ice water to stop the cooking.

To make mousseline sauce, place vinegar, cracked pepper, ½ cup water and egg yolks in the top of a double boiler over boiling water.

Beat the yolks until they thicken, then slowly add the warm butter, bit by bit, whisking until sauce is smooth. Whisk in lemon juice, whipped cream and salt and pepper to taste. Makes enough sauce for 5 servings.

Serves 2.

Flambees de Bananes Martiniquaise (Flamed Bananas Martinique-Style)

- 4 bananas
- 2 ounces (4 tablespoons) butter, melted
- 2 ounces brown sugar
- 1 teaspoon ground cinnamon
- Juice of 2 oranges
- 2 ounces raisins
- ½ cup rum
- 2 servings ice cream

Peel bananas and split lengthwise. Mix melted butter with brown sugar and cinnamon in a saute pan and saute the bananas 2 minutes on both sides. Add orange juice and raisins. At the last minute, flame with rum. Serve over dark chocolate ice cream.

Serves 2.

La Tour d'Argent
2011 Ella Blvd. & T.C. Jester
Houston, Texas 77008
864-9864

Les Continents/ The Brasserie

FAVORITES

Earl Grey Sour
Kiwi Ginger Sparkle
Fillet of Redfish Wrapped in Lettuce Leaves
*Baby Chicken Mercado
With Cilantro Lime Butter*
*Beef Tenderloin Tips in Green Peppercorn
Cream Sauce With Garlic Fried Rice*
Glazed Strawberry Dessert Soup
Strawberry Cheesecake

A relative newcomer on the scene, Hotel Inter-Continental, which opened in 1984, quickly established a reputation for gourmet dining experiences on various levels.

Les Continents is the premier specialty restaurant used for private parties, corporate entertaining, gourmet events and vintner dinners. The Brasserie is more informal, but offers some of the same menu items.

The elements of fine design, furnishings and fine food come together to create a pleasant atmosphere whether one's schedule allows only a quick breakfast or mid-day meal or a leisurely dinner.

Executive chef Helmut Sussenbach draws on his considerable talents and experience developed in Inter-Continental hotels all over the world to produce contemporary food in the grand style.

A native of West Germany, the chef began his career at 14, and has traveled around the world including two years as a chef on a luxury liner.

His eclectic international menus are a mixture of classical and contemporary dishes based on fresh and unique regional ingredients. Among his more innovative dishes are Texas Jack Rabbit Sausage With Spicy Lingonberry Jelly, Fresh Wisconsin Duck Liver With Essence of Raspberry Vinegar, Honey Glazed Washington State Rack of Lamb, Cream of Escargot Soup and Tapioca Yogurt Pudding With Mango Sauce.

However, the classics such as Dover sole, salmon, Caesar salad, beef, fine steaks and veal dishes are not neglected.

Star Attractions

★ Convenient location in the heart of Galleria.

★ The Brasserie, a two-level dining area with atrium and skylights which offers varied dining choices from breakfast to Sunday brunch, a la carte meals, elaborate holiday brunch buffets. Twenty-four hour room service and bar lounge available for hotel guests.

★ Quiet, relaxed setting.

★ Bread basket includes six types of breads and rolls made in-house.

★ Breakfast specialties including Cream of Wheat, oatmeal, muesli cereals and an assortment of muffins, croissants and pastries baked in-house.

★ Menus feature several heart healthy dishes that meet American Heart Association guidelines; skim milk and dishes modified to omit fat, salt, etc. on request. Brasserie features delicious non-alcoholic drinks.

★ Oktoberfest, a boisterous annual beer-and-sausage festival that coincides with the original festival in Munich with oompah bands and beer imported from Germany. New this year will be non-alcoholic German beer.

★ Large selection of wines.

★ Recognition by wine and food societies. The hotel and restaurant have been the setting for dinners of the Confrerie des Chaine des Rotisseurs (of which the chef is a member), International Wine and Food Society, Commanderie de Bordeaux and Foods and Wine of France.

★ Conference and Exhibition Center, a 20,000-square-foot facility for trade shows, public events and other large gatherings; serves 1,600 for seated dinners.

★ Involvement in many civic and social projects and benefits. The hotel participates in the Food Loop program of the End Hunger Network.

Earl Grey Sour

- 10 ounces brewed Earl Grey ice tea
- 6 ounces sweet/sour mix (see Note)
- 2 cups crushed ice
- Lemon wedges for garnish

Combine ingredients and blend in blender. Garnish glasses with a lemon wedge and cherry.

Note: Sweet/sour mix is available at liquor and bar-supply shops.

Serves 4.

Kiwi Ginger Sparkle

- ½ kiwifruit, peeled
- 1 peach slice, peeled
- ½ cup crushed ice
- Chilled ginger ale
- Kiwi slice and maraschino cherry for garnish

Blend kiwi, peach slice, sweet/sour mix and crushed ice to a slush in blender. Pour into stemmed glass and fill with ginger ale. Garnish with slice of kiwi and a cherry.

Serves 1.

Fillet of Redfish Wrapped in Lettuce Leaves

- 6 romaine leaves, blanched
- 1 redfish fillet per person (2 pounds fillets will serve 6)
- Juice of ½ lemon
- Worcestershire sauce (1 tablespoon per serving)
- Salt and pepper
- 3 tablespoons minced shallots
- 3 tablespoons butter
- 3 cups champagne
- 1 pint (2 cups) whipping cream
- 1 recipe Hollandaise sauce (to serve 6)
- 6 tablespoons whipped heavy cream
- 6 fleurons (see Note), optional

To blanch lettuce: Drop leaves into boiling water 1 to 2 minutes or just until softened and still bright green; drain and set aside in container of ice water.

Season fish as desired with lemon juice, Worcestershire, salt and pepper. Wrap each fillet in a lettuce leaf, folding ends around to seal. Saute shallots in butter in a saute pan. Place fish in pan; add champagne. Cover and cook (braise) 8 minutes. Remove fish.

Reduce stock until cooked down about three-quarters. Add cream. Reduce until cream and stock mixture thickens, 3 to 4 minutes. Strain sauce.

Ladle sauce on one side of each plate. Place fish in sauce. Fold 6 tablespoons whipped cream into hollandaise and coat each fillet. Place under broiler until glazed golden brown. Garnish plates with baby vegetables and with fleurons as a special touch.

Note: Make fleurons by cutting ⅛-inch thick puff pastry into half moon shapes with a fluted pastry cutter 2 inches long. Brush with beaten egg and bake at 400 degrees 10 minutes.

Serves 4.

Diet Alert: Omit hollandaise.

Baby Chicken Mercado With Cilantro Lime Butter

- 4 pieces deboned baby chicken (poussin) or chicken breast
- Salt and pepper to taste
- Vegetable oil
- 2 ounces each chopped red, green and yellow bell peppers
- 2 ounces sliced onion (about ¼ of medium onion)
- 2 ounces sliced fresh mushrooms
- 2 ounces (4 tablespoons) butter
- Salt and pepper to taste

Preheat oven to 400 degrees. Salt and pepper chicken. Brush oil over chicken and place on roasting tray. Roast in preheated 400-degree oven 15 minutes, then check for doneness. Larger pieces may take longer.

Saute peppers, onion and mushrooms in butter and season with salt and pepper.

Cilantro Lime Butter
- 4 ounces (1 stick) butter
- 2 ounces fresh lime juice
- 1 ounce chopped cilantro leaves
- Salt and pepper to taste

Melt butter in frying pan over low heat. Add lime juice, stirring constantly until creamy. Season with salt and pepper and add cilantro leaves.

Place chicken on hot dinner plate and top with sauteed vegetables and cilantro lime butter.

Serves 4.

Beef Tenderloin Tips in Green Peppercorn Cream Sauce With Garlic Fried Rice

- 1¾ pounds beef tenderloin, sliced and cut in strips
- Salt and pepper
- 2 ounces clarified butter or vegetable oil
- 2 ounces (about 4 tablespoons) chopped shallots or onions
- 1 ounce (2 tablespoons) whole green peppercorns
- 2 tablespoons prepared mustard
- 1 ounce Cognac (the chef prefers Remy Martin)
- ½ cup brown gravy (make your own or use canned or mix)
- ¾ cup heavy (whipping) cream

Season the meat with salt and pepper. Heat a skillet over high heat; add half the butter and heat. Sear the meat in hot butter to seal in juices; remove meat from skillet and set aside.

Heat remaining butter in same skillet and saute the shallots, green peppercorns and mustard. Carefully flame with Cognac. Add the brown gravy and let simmer to reduce. Add the sauteed meat to the sauce and finish with heavy cream. Season to taste with salt and pepper.

Garlic Fried Rice
- 4 cups cooked rice
- 3 ounces (1 small head) chopped garlic
- 2 ounces clarified butter
- Salt and pepper

Saute the garlic in the butter. Add rice. Season with salt and pepper.

Serves 4.

Glazed Strawberry Dessert Soup

- 1¼ pounds strawberries, washed, dried, hulled and sliced
- 3 ounces orange liqueur
- 3 ounces kirschwasser (clear cherry brandy)
- 2 cups sugar
- 6 egg yolks
- 10 ounces white wine

In medium mixing bowl mix strawberries, orange liqueur, kirschwasser and 1 cup sugar. Cover mixture and refrigerate at least 1 hour to marinate while making sauce.

In heavy saucepan over very low heat, slowly whip egg yolks, 1 cup sugar and wine until mixture thickens and will coat the back of a wooden spoon. Spoon strawberry mixture into individual glasses and pour sauce over top. Run under the broiler just until lightly browned.

Serves 4.

Strawberry Cheesecake

- 3 pounds cream cheese, softened
- 2¼ cups sugar
- Vanilla extract
- Lemon zest (barest yellow peel)
- 1 envelope (1 ounce) unflavored gelatin dissolved in 3 tablespoons cold water
- 3 cups heavy whipping cream, whipped
- ½ pound fresh strawberries, cleaned, hulled and pureed
- 1 baked sponge cake, cut in half horizontally
- Strawberry marmalade or jam

Beat cream cheese, sugar, few drops of vanilla extract and 2 tablespoons lemon zest on slow speed of electric mixture. Mix in dissolved gelatin, then whipped cream.

Mix in pureed strawberries. Place 1 layer of sponge cake in the bottom of a 9-inch springform pan. Spread marmalade over sponge cake. Fill mold with cream cheese-strawberry mixture. Refrigerate until set, at least 1 to 2 hours.

Remove sides of pan, turn cake out of pan upside down, then turn, cheesecake side up, onto serving tray. Decorate with whipped cream and fresh strawberries fans. Cut in wedges to serve. Chopped almonds or nuts on outside.

Les Continents/The Brasserie
Hotel Inter-Continental
5150 Westheimer
Houston, Texas 77056
961-1500

Louisiana Don's

FAVORITES

Snapper Courtbouillon
Cajun Stuffed Pork Roast
Crawfish Etouffee
Shrimp and Avocado Salad
Blueberry Cheesecake
Louisiana Meringue Bread Pudding

Recently refurbished and redecorated, Don's Seafood is also revising its name and its image. As Louisiana Don's it is turning up the energy level for good times in the spirit of a Mardi Gras party that goes on all year long.

The Galleria area restaurant has livened things up with Mardi Gras colors of purple, green and gold, feathered Mardi Gras masks, confetti, photographs, posters, real musical instruments and a revised menu.

As you enter, a fresh fish and seafood case draws attention to the oyster bar, a good place to meet friends for drinks and a light meal or snack of fresh oysters or other seafood. White louvered shutter windows, white tile floors and walls with a blue tile border detail carry through the fish market atmosphere.

New additions include a patio with a pleasant view of the waterwall fountain at the Transco Tower across the street and a glassed-in private dining room for 25 in the heart of the restaurant.

Owned by the same Louisiana Cajuns who bring you Magnolia Bar and Grill and Jimmy G's (Jody Larriviere, Jimmy Gossett and Floyd Landry), Louisiana Don's is concentrating on the good tastes of Louisiana cooking.

Louisiana favorites from Dixieland to Zydeco music are playing in the background as you enjoy Louisiana favorites from the kitchen—fresh fish, seafood and traditional home-style dishes such as gumbo, etouffee and pecan pie.

Old favorites remain on the menu, which also features a new sauteed seafood dish of shrimp, scallops, crab fingers, lump crab and crawfish tails baked in ramekins with a garlic butter.

Sundays you find such specials as stuffed pork roast, a boneless fresh pork ham stuffed with a fresh vegetable mixture and roasted.

During Mardi Gras, Louisiana Don's will feature traditional dishes such as King's Cake.

Star Attractions

★ Location convenient to Galleria and Summit arena.

★ Convenient hours: open seven days a week, 11 a.m. to 10 p.m. Monday through Thursdays and Sunday; to 11 p.m. Friday and Saturday.

★ Cajun and other regional specialties—etouffees, crawfish pie, softshell crab and even alligator in season.

★ Varied dining settings: Oyster bar; outside patio with view of the Transco Tower waterwall; private dining room; dining areas on different levels.

★ Sunday brunch from 11 a.m. to 2:30 p.m. featuring Louisiana specialties.

★ Catering and take-out available. Home delivery (call for information).

★ Good wine list; wines by the glass; traditional Louisiana drinks like Hurricanes.

★ Donate food to the End Hunger project sponsored by the End Hunger Network.

Snapper Courtbouillon

- 2 pounds red snapper fillets
- ¼ cup light oil
- ¼ cup flour
- 4 (1-pound) cans tomatoes, squeezed and drained
- ½ cup diced onion
- ¼ cup diced celery
- ¼ cup diced bell pepper
- 2 cloves garlic
- 1 quart fish or chicken stock or water
- ½ cup chopped green onion
- ¼ cup chopped fresh parsley
- 1 lemon, cut into 6 thin slices

Heat black iron skillet to medium high temperature. Make a roux: Add oil, stir in flour and cook until brown, stirring continuously with flat end of metal spatula or whisk, about 40 minutes (or make in microwave—see Roux in Special Helps section).

Add tomatoes, onions and celery; cook until tender. Add bell pepper and garlic; cook 5 minutes.

Add stock and simmer 30 minutes until sauce will coat a spoon. Add snapper fillets and simmer 15 to 20 minutes.

Just before serving, add green onions, parsley and lemon slices to top. Serve with rice.

Serves 6 to 8.

Crawfish Etouffee

- 2 sticks (1 cup) butter
- 3 medium onions, finely chopped
- 6 ribs celery, finely chopped
- 2 cloves garlic, mashed and chopped
- 2 pounds cleaned crawfish tails
- 1 cup chicken stock
- Salt and cayenne pepper to taste
- ¼ cup each chopped green onion tops and fresh parsley

Heat large saucepan and melt butter in it; add onion, celery and garlic; cook until vegetables are tender. Add crawfish tails to vegetable mixture; stir in chicken stock. Add salt and cayenne pepper to taste.

Reduce heat to medium low. Cover and simmer 20 minutes. Add green onion and parsley. Cook 2 minutes longer. Serve with rice. Great with garlic bread.

Serves 4 to 6.

Diet Alert: Spray saucepan with non-stick spray; use diet margarine or reduce butter to ½ cup or less. use de-fatted, unsalted chicken broth.

Shrimp and Avocado Salad

- 1 pound boiled, peeled shrimp
- 5 ribs celery, diced
- ¼ cup each diced black and green olives
- 1 small green bell pepper, diced
- 1 small red bell pepper, diced
- 4 hard-boiled eggs, diced
- Juice of ½ lemon
- ¾ cup mayonnaise (can use light)
- 1 tablespoon sweet relish
- Salt, pepper and cayenne to taste
- 1 bunch leaf lettuce
- 1 head iceberg lettuce, torn in pieces
- 2 tomatoes, cut into wedges
- 2 avocados, cut into wedges
- 1 lemon, cut into wedges
- Chopped parsley

Combine shrimp, celery, olives, bell pepper, diced eggs, lemon juice, mayonnaise, relish, salt, pepper and cayenne. Mix well and chill 2 to 3 hours before serving.

To serve, line 6 to 8 bowls with leaf lettuce, then fill with iceberg lettuce. Place a 4-ounce portion of salad mixture on each bed of lettuce. Garnish with wedges of tomato, avocado, lemon and parsley.

Serves 6 to 8.

Diet Alert: Use light mayonnaise and only 2 eggs.

Cajun Stuffed Pork Roast

Featured as a special on Louisiana Don's Sunday brunch menu.

- 1 (8-pound) boneless pork roast (fresh pork ham or front shoulder)

Stuffing Mix:
- 1 large onion, cut in chunks
- 1 small green bell pepper, cut in chunks
- 5 cloves garlic
- Zest of ½ lemon (barest yellow peel only)
- 1 rib celery, cut in pieces
- Salt and pepper (about 1 teaspoon each)
- 1 teaspoon cayenne pepper

Preheat oven to 325 degrees. Combine onion, bell pepper, garlic, lemon zest, celery, salt, pepper and cayenne in large food processor (or do in batches). Process until ingredients are finely chopped.

Using a paring knife, make several deep slits around the perimeter of the roast. Using your index finger, insert three-quarters of stuffing mix into slits. Place roast in baking pan and rub exterior of roast with mix.

Combine the remaining mix with ⅛ inch of water in baking pan. Place in preheated oven. Basting often, about every 20 to 30 minutes, cook to an internal temperature of 165 degrees on a meat thermometer.

Serves 12.

Blueberry Cheesecake

Graham Cracker Pecan Crust
1½ cups graham cracker crumbs
¼ cup finely chopped pecans
¼ cup brown sugar
3 tablespoons melted butter

Combine all ingredients and mix well. Firmly pack mixture onto bottom of a 9-inch springform pan. Bake 12 minutes at 350 degrees. Let cool.

Filling
1 pound cream cheese, softened
1 cup sugar
3 egg whites
1 tablespoon fresh lemon juice
3 cups sour cream
2 teaspoons vanilla extract

Mix cheese and sugar in electric mixer until smooth and creamy. Slowly add egg whites, lemon juice, sour cream and vanilla. Pour mixture over crust in springform pan. Refrigerate until firm.

Blueberry Topping
16 ounces fresh or frozen blueberries
1 tablespoon sugar
1 ounce creme de cassis liqueur

Combine ingredients in saucepan and cook over medium heat until sauce thickens. Let cool and refrigerate.

To serve, cut cheesecake in wedges and spoon topping over it. Canned blueberry pie filling may be used as a topping.

Diet Alert: Reduce brown sugar in crust to 2 tablespoons and use diet margarine instead of butter. Use light cream cheese and sugar substitute equal to 1 cup sugar, or use half sugar-half sugar substitute. Substitute light sour cream or plain non-fat yogurt for sour cream, or use vanilla non-fat yogurt instead of sour cream and vanilla.

Louisiana Meringue Bread Pudding

An impressive meringue-topped bread pudding. Nine cups sounds like a lot of milk, but the amount is correct. The bread pudding fills a 13x9x2-inch baking dish and rises to the top of the pan or above as it bakes; it makes enough to feed a party. After baking, it is topped by meringue and browned in the oven.

8 eggs, separated
1 cup sugar plus 2 to 3 tablespoons
9 cups milk
4 teaspoons vanilla extract
8 hamburger buns, broken up
½ cup raisins
½ cup chopped pecans
   Pinch of cinnamon and nutmeg
¼ pound (8 tablespoons) butter

Preheat oven to 325 degrees. Beat egg yolks and 1 cup sugar until creamy; add milk and vanilla extract. Add crumbled hamburger buns, raisins, pecans, cinnamon and nutmeg.

Cut pats of butter and place at bottom of a 13x9x2-inch baking pan. Add mixture. Bake at 325 degrees 50 to 70 minutes or until knife comes out clean when inserted in center of pudding.

Beat egg whites until foamy. Beat in 2 to 3 tablespoons sugar gradually until meringue holds its shape, but is not dry. Spread meringue on baked bread pudding and place under broiler until meringue is lightly browned.

Notes: if using glass pan, spread meringue on pudding and bake in 375-degree oven until browned instead of putting under broiler. In place of raisins and pecans, use your favorite fruit.

Diet Alert: Skim milk and egg substitute may be used and butter may be reduced to 6 tablespoons.

*Louisiana Don's
3009 South Post Oak
Houston, Texas 77056
629-5380*

Prego

FAVORITES

*Roasted Poblano Crab Cakes With
Lemon Caper Tomato Mayonnaise*

Grilled Chicken Salad

*South of the Border Fettucini With
Grilled Chicken and Black Beans*

*Summery Linguini With Black Beans,
Corn, Coriander and Tomato Sauce*

*Grilled Lamb Chops With
Pink Peppercorn Sauce*

Prego's "Italian and Southwestern" cuisine may sound a bit incongruous—until you taste the results of the innovative melding of the two cuisines—fettucini flavored with jalapenos; lamb chops marinated in olive oil and Italian herbs such as oregano, basil and rosemary; corn, black beans and cilantro added to linguini with a cream sauce, or sauteed prawns with red peppers and prosciutto.

Tracy Lee Vaught, who owns Backstreet Cafe, took over as general manager for Prego's new owners in early 1988, and they are revamping the restaurant and menu to appeal to a wider innercity clientele.

The casual neighborhood restaurant in the Rice University Village seats 65, with a small wine room for overflow or private parties. The restaurant attracts a mixed crowd of varying ages from West University Place, the Texas Medical Center and surrounding neighborhoods as well as the innercity.

The long, narrow restaurant is visually defined by a beautifully carved bar opposite a wall of banquettes, and the pressed tin ceiling.

Pink, peach and dark evergreen are the base colors of the decor and appear in everything from spatter-painted walls to flamestitch upholstery fabrics on the banquettes and Fiestaware pottery.

Walls are hung with a changing exhibit of paintings that come and go as they are sold.

Chef Brian Drennan, a native Houstonian, started cooking in his Cuban grandmother's kitchen in Beaumont when he was 8.

After high school, he graduated from the Culinary Institute of America in Hyde Park, New York, in 1982. At the CIA he became well-grounded in classic cooking and techniques. However, he likes to experiment and in his "Italian and Southwestern cuisine" he feels he is combining the best of both worlds.

Prego specializes in pasta, chicken, fish and seafood (including escargot, mussels and calamari), pizza and calzone (Italian sandwiches which resemble stuffed pizzas), grilled dishes and salads. A Lite Lunch menu offers a soup of the day, salads and several distinctive sandwiches such as grilled sausage with peppers and onions, eggplant Parmesan and grilled chicken breast with avocado and red onion.

Among signature grilled dishes is a cheese appetizer of buffalo milk Mozzarella with basil leaf, wrapped in prosciutto, grilled and topped with sun dried tomato vinaigrette.

Popular nighttime entrees are prawns, fettucini with garlic and linguini tossed with vegetables and herbs.

Star Attractions

★ Convenient location near the Texas Medical Center, the Astrodome, Rice University, River Oaks, Montrose and the innercity. Convenient for before-game or -event dining.

★ Casual atmosphere. Open seven nights a week for dinner and Monday through Friday for lunch.

★ Creative Italian and Southwestern cuisine that blends the best products and tastes of both cuisines. Nightly chef's specials. Delicious breads, including small Italian loaves, made in-house. Fresh pastas custom-made to specifications.

★ Variety of pizzas and calzones made in stone baking ovens.

★ Heart-healthy dishes (a small heart marks menu items that are low-fat and low-cholesterol). Accommodate requests for no salt or butter; feature a non-egg pasta.

★ Half orders of most pasta dishes available.
★ Take-out or delivery (call for information).
★ Wine room for private parties (accommodates 12). Can arrange to reserve restaurant for private parties on Mondays.
★ Dessert tray features custom Descours Desserts from pastry chef Marilyn Descours. Temptations include Blackout cake, coconut cream pie and chocolate caramel torte, espresso, cappuccino and other after-dinner coffees.
★ Good wine list; many served by the glass.
★ Known for martinis served in big glasses, the bar features specialty drinks created for the restaurant. Among them: the Ascot (Champagne and Pimm's), Silver Bullet (Stolichnaya vodka and Rumple Minze peppermint liqueur), Peppar Mary (bloody mary made with Absolut peppar vodka), Zipper (brandy, Chamboard liqueur and fruit juice) and Blue Marlin (brandy, blue Curacao and lime juice).

Roasted Poblano Crab Cakes

- 1 large poblano pepper, roasted and peeled
- ½ pound cleaned, shelled lump crabmeat (see Chef's Tips)
- 1 medium tomato, chopped
- 1 tablespoon each minced shallot and garlic
- 2 eggs
- 1½ cups unseasoned bread crumbs (such as Chinese crumbs from Paris Gourmet bakery)
- ½ cup chopped fresh parsley
- 1½ cups mayonnaise
  Dash each of bottled red pepper sauce and Worcestershire
  Salt and pepper to taste
  Juice of 1 lemon
- 4 ounces clarified butter
  Lemon Caper Tomato Mayonnaise (recipe follows)

Mince roasted poblano pepper and place in mixing bowl with crab, tomato, shallot, garlic, eggs, bread crumbs, parsley and mayonnaise.

Add pepper sauce and Worcestershire, salt, pepper and lemon juice. Form into small patties.

Heat non-stick skillet, then heat clarified butter. Carefully add crabcakes and cook on both sides until golden brown. Serve with Lemon Caper Tomato Mayonnaise.

Serves 2.

Chef's Tips: Less expensive crab claws, snow crab or smaller pieces may be substituted for lump crab. See Special Helps section on clarifying butter and roasting peppers.

Lemon Caper Tomato Mayonnaise
- ¼ cup capers, drained
- ½ cup chopped tomato
  Juice of 1 lemon
- 3 cups mayonnaise

Combine capers, tomato, lemon juice and mayonnaise; mix well. Can also be used with grilled chicken sandwich or other mayonnaise dishes.

Diet Alert: Reduce amount of butter; spray pan with non-stick spray. Use light mayonnaise.

Grilled Chicken Salad

Hot grilled chicken breasts (allow half a breast per person), cut into strips
- ½ head red tip lettuce
- 1 head radicchio
- 1 large bunch watercress
- 1 head Belgian endive
- ½ cup fresh mint leaves
- ½ cup extra-virgin olive oil
- ¼ cup raspberry vinegar
- ½ cup coarsely chopped walnuts
- ½ cup crumbled blue cheese such as Gorgonzola

Salt and pepper to taste
Red onion rings for garnish

Wash and clean all vegetables. Core romaine and radicchio and tear into bite-size pieces (see Chef's Tips that follow).

Clean and strip leaves from watercress. Peel off outer endive leaves and discard if wilted; separate leaves.

In a mixing bowl, whisk together mint, oil, raspberry vinegar, walnuts and salt and pepper. Lightly toss with vegetables and chicken strips.

Arrange endive in a star design on outer edge of two plates. Place salad on plate. Top with blue cheese and onion rings.

Chef's Tips: To grill chicken breasts, brush first with herbs and a little oil. To core radicchio easily, smack on the counter on core end and pop out the core as you would iceberg lettuce. If radicchio is unavailable, substitute shredded red cabbage.

South of the Border Fettucini With Grilled Chicken and Black Beans

- 2½ cups diced grilled chicken breast (about 1 boneless chicken breast per person)
- Butter
- 1 cup seeded, crushed fresh tomatoes (about 2 medium tomatoes)
- ½ cup cooked black beans
- 1 cup chopped cilantro leaves
- 1 tablespoon minced jalapeno
- ½ tablespoon (1½ teaspoons) minced garlic
- 2 ounces (⅛ cup) white wine
- 2 ounces (⅛ cup) chicken stock

Salt and pepper to taste
- 8 ounces fresh jalapeno fettucini

Cilantro leaves and tomato wedges for garnish

In a medium saute pan, heat 4 tablespoons clarified butter. Add tomato, black beans, cilantro, jalapeno and garlic and saute 3 to 5 minutes. Pour off all but a tablespoon or two of accumulated fat if any; add grilled chicken.

Deglaze pan with white wine (add wine and simmer, scraping up any browned bits from the bottom with a wooden spoon).

Add chicken stock and let simmer until reduced by one-fourth. Add salt and pepper to taste.

Bring a large pot of water to a boil. Drop pasta into boiling water and cook 2½ to 3 minutes, until of the desired consistency. Drain.

Add 2 ounces cold butter to sauce and stir it in until sauce looks creamy. To serve: place pasta on plate or in shallow bowl; top with sauce. Garnish with cilantro leaves and tomato wedges if desired.

Serves 2.

The chef recommends serving this with Italian bread and cold beer.

Diet alert: Reduce amount of butter or use diet margarine; omit 2 ounces cold butter at end.

Summery Linguini With Black Beans, Corn, Cilantro and Tomato Sauce for Two

- 2 medium tomatoes
- 1 ear fresh corn, husked
- ½ pound linguini
- 1 egg
- 1 tablespoon red wine vinegar
- ½ teaspoon sugar
- Salt and pepper to taste
- 1 tablespoon full-flavored olive oil
- ⅓ cup minced cilantro leaves
- ½ small red onion, chopped
- ½ cup cooked black beans (can use canned), drained

Bring a large pot of water to a boil. Drop in the tomatoes and corn and let the water return to a boil. Remove tomatoes with a slotted spoon after 30 seconds. Let corn boil 1½ minutes longer. Remove corn, cover pot and keep the water at a low boil.

Peel and seed tomatoes, cut into ½-inch dice. Cut the corn kernels off the cob. Drop the linguini into the boiling water and cook until barely tender.

Meanwhile, whirl egg in a food processor until light and fluffy. Add half the diced tomato, the vinegar, sugar, salt and pepper to taste. Whirl to blend.

Drain pasta and toss with olive oil in a hot skillet or serving dish. Add cilantro, black beans, onion and corn. Add the tomato-egg sauce and toss until pasta is coated. Toss to mix. Serve hot with freshly grated Pamesan. A good wine accompaniment is Pinot Grigio.

Serves 2.

Grilled Lamb Chops With Pink Peppercorn Sauce

- 4 (4½-ounce) lamb chops (Colorado lamb if available)
- 1 cup extra-virgin olive oil
- 1 chopped onion
- ½ cup each fresh oregano, fresh rosemary and fresh basil, cleaned and chopped
- Salt and pinch of white pepper
- 1 ounce (2 tablespoons) clarified butter
- 1 cup chopped red onion (1 medium)
- ¼ cup pink peppercorns
- 1½ ounces brandy
- 2 ounces (⅛ cup) heavy whipping cream

Marinate lamb chops overnight in combined olive oil, chopped onion, herbs and salt and pepper.

Heat a grill to medium hot. Place chops on grill and cook to desired doneness.

Meanwhile, in a saucepan, heat 2 tablespoons clarified butter. Saute red onion and peppercorns being careful not to burn. Deglaze pan: Add brandy and cream and stir up any browned bits at bottom of pan. Salt to taste. Simmer sauce until reduced by one-fourth and thickened.

Place chops on plate and serve with sauce.

Serves 2.

Recommended wine accompaniment is a full-bodied Chianti such as Ruffino Gold.

Prego
2520 Amherst
Houston, Texas 77005
529-2420

Quail Hollow Inn

> ### FAVORITES
> *Chinese Chicken Salad With
> Honey Ginger Dressing
> Flounder With Lime
> Quail With Apples
> Quail Hunters' Delicacy
> (oysters, shrimp stew)
> Cheesecake*

Quail Hollow Inn is one part Swiss chalet, one part Texas country lodge and one part gourmet restaurant. The three elements add up to a fine dining experience keyed to the personality of the chef/owner, Karl Caminzind.

Caminzind comes from a Swiss hotel family; two uncles were executive chefs, and his father owned a butcher shop in Switzerland where Karl began apprenticing at 15. He ran the business for a few years, then worked in London before coming to the U.S. in 1962.

Caminzind says he prepares what he likes, but the menu has wide appeal because people drive from as far away as the Woodlands, Spring and Galveston to dine there.

His repertoire still includes traditional favorites he prepared in Europe. Many are dishes that are difficult to find at other restaurants—Beef Wellington, Shirred Eggs in Cocotte, Reuben sandwiches (many guests think Quail Hollow's version is the best Reuben around), Pork Schnitzel, Wiener Schnitzel, Coq au Vin and Sweetbreads with Spaetzle.

Other menu items are from Caminzind's stints as a hotel chef with the Biltmore in Arizona, Hilton in California and New Orleans, and as executive chef of the Marriott in Denver. He likes to use local regional ingredients and one dish he considers a "must" on the menu is that Texas classic, Chicken Fried Steak.

He is not into nouvelle cuisine, Caminzind says, but he has lightened many dishes and sauces (few are flour-thickened), uses very little salt, now serves margarine instead of butter, features a lot of fresh fish and chicken and will modify dishes for special diets on request.

The menu also includes contemporary surprises such as Blue Marlin with a Sweet Pepper Sauce, Mahi Mahi and Veal Dijon.

The chef and his wife Susie first looked around in Houston for a restaurant site but decided they liked the more relaxed atmosphere of Richmond, which on a good traffic day is only a half-hour drive from the Galleria and Summit areas. They also saw a great potential in growing developments nearby such as Pecan Grove, Sugar Land and Missouri City.

They opened the restaurant in December, 1985, in a refurbished red brick building dating to 1883. It had been a department store and a feed store, then fallen into neglect. The windows had even been covered with stucco over the brick.

They gave the old building a new lease on life by restoring the windows, adding cabinetry, parquet dados to walls and ceiling fans with etched glass light globes. They repainted and refurbished, adding the Alpine touch of shuttered windows and flower boxes filled with red geraniums and plants. The restaurant seats 92, partly on a raised gallery area opposite the windows. The back bar, with a sports bar atmosphere, seats 45. An upstairs room accommodates up to 150 for banquets and private parties.

Stained glass panels and light catchers (ask, they're for sale) were made by Susie's uncle who also made the stained glass and metal candleholders for each table. The decor includes walls hung with paintings, photographs of Swiss scenes familiar to Caminzind and chiming clocks; one cabinet holds a collection of quails in china, wood and other materials; many are gifts from customers.

Lunch draws the crowd from nearby businesses and the county court house. The Sunday buffet brunch from 11:30 a.m. to 2 p.m. gets big play from loyal customers and visiting city folks. They have discovered that Quail Hollow Inn is the perfect little getaway for a leisurely meal.

Star Attractions

★ Casual, homey atmosphere; moderate prices.

★ House specials including Quail in a Nest (two quails on artichoke bottom with chestnut puree and Marsala sauce), Steak & Quail (grilled filet mignon with quail dipped in teriyaki sauce), Quail & Shrimp (grilled quail with deep-fried shrimp in a beer batter), roast duckling and veal dishes.

★ Happy hour from 4 to 7 p.m. weekdays with free hors d'oeuvre. Pianist on Friday and Saturday nights.

★ Birthday and anniversary mementos—a free dessert and souvenir Polaroid photo. One couple, who had their first date at Quail Hollow, come back every year to celebrate their wedding anniversary.

★ Children's menu featuring grilled pork chop, fried shrimp or roast beef.

★ Catering from full meals and barbecues to birthday cakes. Also take-out.

★ Sunday buffet brunch—a groaning board of vegetable and fruit salads, marinated salmon, pickled asparagus, okra and relishes, vegetables, blintzes, made-to-order omelets, roast beef and prime rib, several entrees and cheeses.

The dessert table includes apple strudel with brandied cream; white chocolate, almond amaretto, lemon and chocolate mousses, fruit and cheesecakes.

★ Open for brunch Christmas Day.

★ Small, but hand-picked wine list including three Swiss wines when available—Fendant, Neuchatel and Dole.

Directions from downtown Houston: Take the Southwest Freeway (Highway 59) west to Highway 6, right on Highway 6 to Alternate 90; turn left and drive 7 miles to Richmond; cross the Brazos River; turn right at the second traffic light (3rd Street); go 1 block (restaurant is on the northeast corner).

Chinese Chicken Salad

- 2 chicken breasts, skinned and boned
- 1 teaspoon ground ginger
- 2 teaspoons dried English mustard
- ¼ cup clarified butter
- ½ to 1 head romaine lettuce
- 2 ounces fresh bean sprouts
- 14 to 16 fresh or frozen snow peas, uncooked
- ¼ cup cashews
- 10 water chestnuts, sliced
- ½ cup dry Chinese noodles (chow mein noodles)
- Honey-Ginger Dressing (recipe follows)

Cut chicken breasts into ½ inch strips; season with ginger and dry mustard. Heat butter in non-stick skillet and saute chicken 2 to 3 minutes (or use part butter and 1 tablespoon sesame oil).

Tear lettuce into bite-size pieces. Sprinkle bean sprouts, snow peas, cashews and water chestnuts over lettuce.

Add hot chicken to salad just before serving. Add Chinese noodles and toss with dressing. Serve immediately.

Serves 2.

Honey Ginger Dressing
- 2 tablespoons raspberry vinegar
- 1 teaspoon prepared yellow mustard
- ½ teaspoon ground ginger
- 4 tablespoons honey
- 1 teaspoon sugar
- ⅛ teaspoon each: cracked pepper, snipped chives, nutmeg and Worcestershire sauce
- 1 tablespoon peanut oil

Whip all ingredients together except oil. Slowly add oil whisking with a wire whip to bind.

Flounder With Lime

4	thin flounder fillets
	Seasoning—chopped fresh tarragon, chopped parsley, garlic powder, salt, white pepper and dill
1½	limes
½	cup demi-glace (brown sauce)
¼	cup clarified butter or margarine
	Flour for coating the fish

Heat butter in saute pan. Season flounder to taste with above seasonings and coat with flour. Saute approximately 1 to 1½ minutes. Turn fish. Squeeze whole lime over fish. Ladle demi-glace over the fish to coat. Do not overcook. Transfer to warm plate. Arrange slices of lime on top for garnish.

Serves 2.

Quail With Apples

4	(3- to 3½-ounce) boneless quail
	Salt and pepper to taste
½	cup flour
½	cup clarified butter
24	garlic cloves, peeled
1	tart green apple, peeled
2	lemons
4	teaspoons white wine
½	cup demi-glace (brown sauce)
	Parsley, for garnish

Season the quail with salt and pepper; lightly dredge in flour. Saute in ovenproof skillet in butter, skin side down first. Turn and add garlic cloves. Roast in 425-degree oven 12 to 15 minutes, until leg wiggles easily when tested.

Remove pan from oven, place on range over medium heat and add apples to the quail. Squeeze lemon over all and add wine and demi-glace.

Place 2 quail on each plate and pour apples and sauce over them. Garnish with parsley.

Serves 2.

Quail Hunters Delicacy

- 2 demi-loaves bread (small sandwich loaves)
- 2 ounces (4 tablespoons) butter
- 1 teaspoon chopped garlic
- 2 teaspoons chopped shallots
- 6 raw shrimp, cut in pieces
- 6 to 8 oysters
  Dash of fresh dill, tarragon, parsley, chives and salt
- 8 fresh mushrooms, sliced
- 4 teaspoons white wine
- ½ cup Supreme Sauce or chicken gravy

Heat bread in oven. Slice off tops of loaves and hollow out the bread. Reserve tops for covers.

Melt butter in saute pan and add garlic and shallots. Add shrimp, oysters, seasonings, sliced mushrooms, wine and gravy. Bring to a boil and cook 2 minutes. Ladle into hollowed out loaves and cover with top. Serve immediately.

For Supreme Sauce or chicken gravy, make a light roux of butter and flour; add milk and whisk until smooth and thickened. Salt and pepper to taste.

Serves 2.

Cheesecake

Crust
- 2½ ounces butter, melted
- 2 cups graham cracker crumbs

Mix butter and crumbs by hand. Press firmly into bottom and sides of 9-inch springform pan. Add filling and bake at 350 degrees 45 minutes, or until cake tests done when a toothpick is inserted in the middle. Let cool 20 minutes before adding topping.

Filling
- 2½ packages (20 ounces) cream cheese, softened and cut in small chunks
- 2½ cups powdered sugar
  Juice of 2 lemons
- 1½ teaspoons vanilla
- 3 teaspoons brandy
- 4 eggs

Beat cream cheese until smooth. Slowly add powdered sugar and blend until smooth. Add lemon juice, vanilla and brandy and mix until completely blended. Add eggs, one at a time, mixing until blended after each addition. Pour into prepared crust.

Topping
- 1 cup sour cream
- ½ cup powdered sugar

Mix sour cream and powdered sugar until blended. Top filling and bake 10 minutes at 400 degrees.

Remove from oven and let cool on counter about 30 minutes. Cool completely, preferably overnight, in refrigerator, before removing from pan. Serve with fresh berries if desired.

Diet Alert: Substitute light cream cheese for regular and use 2 eggs plus 4 egg whites instead of whole eggs. Substitute plain or non-fat vanilla yogurt for sour cream.

Quail Hollow Inn
241 Morton
Richmond, Texas 77469
341-6733

Rao's Ristorante Italiano & Bar

FAVORITES

Radicchio and Fennel Salad
Tony Rao's Risotto
Involtini de Pollo
Snapper Toto
Ravioli al Sugo

Rao's blends the tastes of Italian tradition with contemporary style to produce memorable dining experiences in a lighthearted setting.

Owner/chef Tony Rao, a native Houstonian, is one of the new breed of Italian chefs who believe in lighter foods and sauces and in combining traditional ingredients in new ways. The menu has been expanded with dishes he discovered while traveling extensively in Italy and includes such regional classics as risotto, osso buco, gnocchi and swordfish.

Although a relative newcomer on the scene, Rao's has already developed a loyal following, many of whom were customers at Rao's former restaurant, D'Amico's.

The new restaurant, which seats 225, opened in May, 1987, in the Greenway Plaza-Summit arena area. Rao's is a family operation; Tony's wife Megan assists with accounting and his younger brother Paul is manager.

From the beginning, Rao has specialized in lighter foods—grilled fish and meats, pasta and appetizers. Almost all are rooted in tradition such as Vitello Tonnatto, sliced cold braised veal with a tuna-caper sauce, a regional specialty of Piedmont; calamari, a regional favorite from the coast of Tuscany, and lasagna (his version is Lasagna Verde made with spinach pasta, a light Bechamel and marinara sauce).

Adding to the restaurant's appeal are the convenient location, unique architecture and pleasing decor in cool shades of peach and sea green. The restaurant occupies a building within a building between the Cashco Tower and Summit Plaza; between the open, airy restaurant and the skylight roof of the building is the metal fretwork of a geodesic dome.

Architectural interest is further enhanced by a painted sea green archway between dining areas, glass windows framed by a contemporary version of Roman columns topped by baskets of trailing ivy, multi-level dining areas and balconies bordered with natural wood. The main dining area gives a view of the fountain plaza between the Coastal and Summit towers across the street.

Dining areas on different levels are almost like stage sets and are lit by hanging handmade fabric-covered parasol lamps.

STAR ATTRACTIONS

★ Convenient location in Greenway Plaza near the Summit for before-event or before-game dining. Rao's is frequented by the Rockets basketball pros and celebrity performers such as Billy Gibbons of ZZ Top, Rod Stewart, Dan Fogelberg, Frankie Avalon and Joan Rivers when they're in town.

★ Specialties such as Snapper Toto with lump crab; Involtini di Pollo (stuffed chicken breasts), homemade pastas and risotto.

★ Custom desserts by Marilyn Descours of Descours Desserts.

★ Catering for groups of 50 to 500. Rao's has catered for celebrities performing at the Summit including Michael Jackson and Frank Sinatra.

★ Take-out of any menu item. Delivery through Dial n Dine (call 877-8777).

★ Private dining room upstairs for wedding rehearsals, receptions and other parties; seats 90. Restaurant available for private parties on Sundays when it's closed.

★ Full service bar. Complimentary hors d'oeuvre at happy hour from 4 to 7 p.m. Monday through Friday.

★ Free valet parking (enter on Colquitt Street, one block north of Richmond between Timmons and Edloe).

Radicchio and Fennel Salad

- 1 pound radicchio
- 2 bunches fresh fennel
- 2 bunches arugula
- ½ pound sliced Parmesan cheese
- ¾ cup extra-virgin olive oil
- ¾ cup balsamic vinegar
- 1 teaspoon coarsely ground black pepper

Cut radicchio, fennel and arugula into bite-size pieces. Cut cheese slices into 1-inch squares.

Mix vegetables and cheese; slowly add oil and vinegar to salad until the desired amount of dressing has been added. Add pepper.

Serves 6.

Tony Rao's Risotto

- 1 quart homemade chicken broth or 1 cup canned broth mixed with 3 cups water
- 2 tablespoons chopped shallots or yellow onion
- 5 tablespoons butter
- 2 tablespoons extra-virgin olive oil
- 2 cups raw Italian Arborio rice
- 10 ounces sliced fresh mushrooms
- ⅓ teaspoon powdered saffron or ½ teaspoon chopped saffron threads dissolved in 1½ cups hot water (optional)*
- 10 ounces fresh green peas or 1 (10-ounce) package frozen green peas
  Salt and pepper to taste
- ¼ cup freshly grated Parmesan cheese (no substitute)

Bring broth to a slow steady simmer in a pot. In a heavy-bottom casserole over medium high heat, saute shallots in 3 tablespoons butter combined with the olive oil.

As shallots become translucent, add rice and stir with a wooden spoon until well coated. Saute 3 minutes, then add ½ cup broth. Continue stirring until rice absorbs the liquid, wiping the sides of the pot as you stir. When rice dries out, add another cup of simmering broth and continue stirring.

You must stir steadily, always loosening the rice from the entire bottom surface of the pot. Otherwise, it will stick badly. Add liquid as rice dries out, but don't drown the rice.

After 15 minutes add the mushrooms and half the saffron if using. Continue cooking rice 10 minutes more, then stir in any other vegetables desired such as fresh asparagus tips, chopped carrots or broccoli florets (cook asparagus and broccoli briefly in the broth, just enough to blanch).

Add peas. The heat of the rice will cook frozen peas and finish cooking asparagus. When rice is tender, but al dente (firm to the bite), taste for seasoning and add salt and pepper as needed.

Add all the cheese and 2 tablespoons softened butter in bits and mix thoroughly. Spoon onto a hot platter and serve with a bowl of freshly grated Parmesan on the side.

*Saffron, the hair-like stigmas of a crocus plant (there are only three per plant) is said to be the most expensive spice in the world today. The threads must be hand-harvested and it takes 75,000 stamen to make one pound. There is no taste substitute, but turmeric is sometimes substituted for color.

Serves 6.

Involtini di Pollo

- 12 chicken breast halves
- 1 (10-ounce) package frozen spinach, thawed
- 1½ pounds Italian sausage
- 1 cup freshly grated Parmesan cheese
- 2 eggs
  - Olive oil
  - Flour
- 1 cup white wine
  - Salt and pepper as needed
- 1 stick (½ cup) butter

Squeeze excess water from spinach. Brown sausage until well done. Break up with a fork. Remove from heat, drain off excess fat and drain on paper towels.

Mix spinach and sausage in a bowl. Add Parmesan and eggs.

Pound chicken breasts to ¼-inch thickness with a mallet. Put a small handful of spinach stuffing in the center of each chicken breast in an oblong shape. Bring the sides of the chicken together and roll up the stuffing to form a cigar-shaped oval.

In a large skillet, heat olive oil over medium high heat. Dust chicken rolls with flour. Saute in hot olive oil until golden brown, about 8 minutes.

Remove from heat and drain off fat. Remove the chicken rolls from skillet. Deglaze pan with white wine and salt and pepper to taste. Add butter and melt, stirring to combine with wine. Add chicken rolls and turn a few times in the sauce. Serve immediately.

Serves 6.

Snapper Toto

- 2 eggs
  - Olive oil
- 6 fresh snapper fillets
  - Flour
- ¾ stick (6 tablespoons) butter
- 1½ pounds jumbo lump crabmeat
- ½ cup pinenuts (pignola)
- ¾ cup dry white wine
- 2 tablespoons chopped fresh parsley
  - Squeeze of fresh lemon juice
  - Fresh parsley and lemon for garnish

Beat eggs in a bowl; set aside. Heat oil in a pan over medium-high heat until just bubbling.

Dip fillets lightly in egg; thoroughly dust with flour. Gently place in hot oil and cook, turning as they are cooked on one side, until they are golden brown, about 6 minutes.

Carefully remove fish from pan and drain on paper towels.

In the same saucepan, melt butter over medium-high heat. Add crab, pinenuts, wine, parsley and a squeeze of lemon juice; simmer 4 to 5 minutes.

Arrange fillets on plates and spoon crab mixture over the fish. Serve immediately.

Serves 6.

Ravioli al Sugo

Pasta
- 1 cup unbleached flour
- 2 large eggs at room temperature
- 1 tablespoon milk

Pour flour onto work surface; shape into a mound and hollow out the center to make a well.

Break eggs into well and add milk. Beat the eggs slightly with a fork 2 minutes. Mix flour and eggs a little at a time, scooping flour in from the edges. Draw the sides of the mound together and work the mixture with your fingers. If too moist, add a little flour, but don't make dough too dry.

Move dough to one side and scrape off all bits of flour and crumbs from work surface. Wash your hands and dry them. Return the dough to work surface and knead with the heel of your palm until dough is thoroughly mixed and smooth.

Flour surface lightly and roll out pasta to desired thinness. Cut dough into 2½-inch wide strips. Cut strips again to form squares.

Set aside on a cloth while preparing stuffing and sauce. Don't put ravioli close enough that they touch or they will stick.

Stuffing
- ½ (10-ounce) package frozen spinach, thawed and squeezed dry
- 1½ cups ricotta cheese
- ½ cup freshly grated Parmesan cheese

Let spinach drain on paper towels. Combine ricotta and Parmesan in large bowl; mix with a fork. Add the dry spinach. Salt and pepper to taste.

Spoon a tablespoon of stuffing mixture in the center of each square. Top with another square of pasta. Pinch edges together. Gently press around edges with a fork to seal.

Sauce
- ¼ cup extra-virgin olive oil
- ½ small garlic clove, peeled and thinly sliced
- 2 pounds (about 10 to 12) ripe Roma tomatoes
- Salt and pepper to taste
- 1 cup finely chopped fresh basil

Heat oil in a large skillet over medium-high heat. Add garlic and cook until garlic turns light brown. Cut tomatoes into small cubes about ¼-inch thick.

Slowly add tomatoes to the oil, stirring constantly. When tomatoes are all in the pot, cover and simmer until the mixture becomes homogenous and oil rises to the top, about 20 minutes. Salt and pepper to taste. Add fresh basil.

Cook the pasta. Heat 4 to 5 quarts water to a rolling boil. Carefully drop in the ravioli a few at a time. Don't drop in too many; they will break.

When tender, but still firm to the tooth, about 4 minutes, remove from the water with a large slotted spoon.

Heat the sauce and pour over the pasta. Serve with grated Parmesan cheese on the side.

Rao's Ristorante Italiano & Bar
#12 Greenway Plaza (3700 Richmond at Edloe)
Houston, Texas 77046
622-8245

Remington on Post Oak Park

FAVORITES

Maryland She Crab Soup With Thyme

Grilled Chicken Ceasar Salad

Warm Spinach Salad With Pancetta Bacon & Sherry Vinaigrette

Stir-Fried Duck With Oriental Vegetables and Sesame Pasta

Seared Gulf Red Snapper With Mint Marigold Sauce and Three Salsas

---

The Remington on Post Oak Park has given Houston a new definition of luxe hotel accommodations and dining. Opened in 1982 at the cost of $200,000 a room, the Remington has changed hands several times, but is still among the hotels that set the standards for fine cuisine and decor.

As demanding connoisseurs would expect, the Remington's imaginative chefs use the freshest and finest products available: mushrooms from Oregon, salad greens picked daily in Oregon and California and sent Federal Express, free-range chickens, Texas blueberries and fresh herbs. The fresh smoked salmon, sausages, pasta, air-dried duck, pates, desserts and chocolates are all done in-house.

One of the nation's young up-and-coming chefs, Peter Rosenberg, directs the kitchen. He began training in Rhodesia when he was 14. A hotel chef in Johannisberg with a reputation as a stern taskmaster instilled in him the principles of formal "silver service" while he worked in the hotel part of the day and in the chef's own restaurant during the afternoons.

He eventually came to America, and earned a degree at the Culinary Institute of America in 1981.

His philosophy of using the best seasonal products and marrying a light, regional style with classic techniques has produced such signature dishes as grilled honey-glazed shrimp with mango black bean chutney; grilled swordfish with jicama, black beans, cilantro and lime and air dried duck with ginger pear sauce.

Rosenberg worked for hotels in California and Memphis before joining Rosewood Hotel Corporation's highly acclaimed Mansion on Turtle Creek in Dallas in 1983. He was executive chef at another Rosewood property, the Bel Air in California, before coming to the Remington in 1987.

Star Attractions

★ Dining in the grand manner with attentive personal service in The Garden Restaurant and glassed-in Conservatory, Bar and Grill or the around pool; 24-hour room service for hotel guests.

★ Emphasis on light, healthful cooking; the chef is attending the Pritikin center to study how to incorporate Pritikin guidelines into meals.

★ Creative cuisine with each dish designed to make the most of the food's natural flavors.

★ Music and dancing with live music on weekends in the Bar and Grill.

★ Gracious surroundings like a luxurious home—handcrafted marble floors, oak paneled walls, stone fireplaces, Dhurrie carpets, original art and antiques. Spectacular flower arrangements. The hotel has been featured in Architectural Digest.

★ Daily tea with harp music in the Living Room which is furnished with elegant pieces beautifully upholstered in velvets and subtle stripes and patterns in soothing neutral colors.

★ Extensive wine cellar with well-rounded international collection.

★ Series of vintner dinners and Wine and Food Weekends matching fine foods and wines.

★ Guest chef series of cooking classes.

★ Outside catering. Can cook and serve special meals in customers' homes.
★ As a courtesy, when regular customers move, complimentary meal and champagne sent to the new house.
★ Power breakfasts popular for business customers.
★ Seated brunch on Saturdays and Sundays; prefixe price.
★ Holds Mobile's four-star rating.
★ Contribute food to the End Hunger Loop project sponsored by the End Hunger Network and support and contribute to many other civic and arts activities.

Maryland She-Crab Soup With Thyme

- ½ cup chopped shallots
- ¼ cup chopped garlic
- 1 quart clam juice
- ½ ounce (about 1 tablespoon) paprika
- 1¼ cups sherry (such as California)
- 1 quart whipping cream
  Pinch of cayenne pepper
  Salt and pepper
- 3 tablespoons cornstarch dissolved in a ¼ cup cold water
- 1 teaspoon fresh thyme
- 8 ounces lump crabmeat

Saute shallots and garlic until softened; add clam juice and paprika and bring to a boil. Add sherry, cream, cayenne, salt and pepper. Dissolve cornstarch in cold water.

Bring soup mixture to a boil, whisk in a little of the cornstarch mixture and simmer until thickened to soup consistency. If too thin, blend in more dissolved cornstarch and whisk until smooth and thick enough to coat the spoon.

Stir in thyme and adjust seasoning with salt and pepper.

Just before serving, fold in crabmeat and reheat gently.

Serves 8.

Stir-Fried Duck With Oriental Vegetables and Sesame Pasta

- 1 tablespoon each sesame and olive oils
- 12 ounces julienned fresh duck meat
- 12 ounces oriental vegetables (see Note)
- 12 ounces sesame fusilli pasta (use plain pasta and saute with a little sesame oil)
- 4 ounces Cooking Marinade (recipe follows)
- 3 teaspoons toasted sesame seeds
- 3 teaspoons black sesame seeds
- 1 scallion flower
  Chilled beet, daikon radish and carrot spirals for garnish

In a very hot skillet heat oils and saute duck and vegetables, tossing and cooking quickly.

Add cooked hot sesame pasta to mix and deglaze with cooking marinade. Adjust seasoning with salt and pepper. Arrange on plate and garnish with scallion flower and sesame seeds.

To make scallion flower, run paring knife vertically along white part of scallion making 6 to 8 cuts around the onion. Trim root end so it fans open when soaked in ice water, about 1 hour.

Cooking Marinade
- 8 ounces soy sauce
- 4 ounces oyster sauce
- 2 ounces sesame oil
- 1 tablespoon grated fresh ginger
- 3 garlic cloves, mashed
- 1 teaspoon chopped shallots
- 1 teaspoon chopped cilantro
- 1 tablespoon chopped chives

In a mixing bowl, combine soy sauce, oyster sauce and sesame oil with wire whisk. Peel and grate ginger, squeeze juice into mix, then add remaining pulp. Add mashed garlic.

Add chopped shallots, cilantro and chives. Mix well and keep refrigerated until needed.

Note: Suggested Oriental Vegetables—carrot, celery, red bell pepper, green bell pepper, green onions, broccoli, cauliflower, zucchini and snow peas. When possible, cut vegetables on the diagonal in Chinese fashion.

Seared Gulf Red Snapper With Mint Marigold Sauce and Three Salsas

- 4 (7-ounce) boned snapper fillets
  Salt and pepper
- 4 ounces Mint Marigold Sauce (recipe follows)
- 4 mint marigold sprigs for garnish (or mix equal parts chopped fresh mint and tarragon)
  Mango Black Bean Salsa, Yellow Bell Pepper Tomato Salsa and Jicama Tomatillo Salsa (recipes follow)

Season snapper with salt and pepper. Sear in hot pan, skin side down. Pour half of Mint Marigold Sauce on plate and place fish skin side up in sauce. Garnish with some of each salsa and a sprig of mint marigold leaf.

Serves 4.

Mint Marigold Sauce
- 2 ounces (⅛ cup) rice wine vinegar
- ¾ cup dry white wine
- 1 garlic clove, chopped
- 1 shallot, chopped
- 1 pound unsalted butter at room temperature
- 2 teaspoons mint marigold leaves (can substitute half chopped fresh mint, half tarragon)
  Salt and pepper

In a saucepan, combine vinegar, wine, garlic and shallot. Cook until reduced to a glaze, about 1 ounce of liquid. Over medium heat, slowly whip in butter until the butter is incorporated or the sauce is thick enough to coat the back of a wooden spoon.

Strain and add chopped mint marigold. Adjust seasoning with salt and pepper. A squeeze of fresh lime might be needed to enhance flavor.

Yellow Bell Pepper Tomato Salsa
- 1 yellow bell pepper, cut in medium dice (about ½ to ¾ cup)
- 4 yellow tomatoes, seeded and diced medium (if unavailable, use more bell pepper, ½ to ¾ cup)
- 2 serrano peppers, seeded and fine diced
- 2 tablespoons diced chives
- 1 teaspoon each: finely chopped garlic, finely chopped shallots, chopped cilantro and chopped fresh parsley
- 2 ounces light colored fruit vinegar
- 1 small red onion, finely diced (about ½ to ¾ cup)

Combine ingredients and adjust seasoning with salt and cayenne pepper.

Jicama Tomatillo Salsa
- 1 medium jicama, cut in small dice (about ¾ cup)
- 2 pounds tomatillos, seeded and diced (about 1 cup)
- 3 jalapenos, seeded and diced finely
- 1 teaspoon cilantro
- 1 teaspoon garlic (2 cloves, chopped)
- 1 teaspoon shallots (1 to 2 shallots, chopped)
  Juice each of 1 lemon and 1 lime
  Salt and pepper to taste
- 2 ounces peanut oil
  Jalapeno vinegar to taste (see Note)

Peel and cut jicama into medium dice. Seed and dice tomatillos (cut ends off, remove insides and dice skins). Cut jalapeno in half, remove seeds and ribs, dice finely.

Chop cilantro, garlic and shallots. Mix all ingredients and adjust seasoning with lemon, lime, salt and pepper. Toss to coat mixture with peanut oil. Correct spiciness and heat of salsa by adding jalapeno vinegar.

Note: To make your own jalapeno vinegar, drop scraps and trimmings from 3 jalapenos into 1 cup white vinegar in a non-aluminum saucepan, bring to a boil, let cool and strain. Let sit until completely cool. Store in refrigerator.

Mango Black Bean Salsa

- 1 green mango (firm and unripe), peeled and diced (2 cups)
- 1 small red bell pepper (about 1 cup diced)
- 1 small red onion (about ½ to ¾ cup, diced)
- 1 chive, sliced
- 1 (3- to 4-inch diameter) jicama, peeled and diced (about 1¼ cups)
- ½ cup (4 ounces) cooked black beans
- 2 ounces honey (2 tablespoons)
- ½ teaspoon ground ginger
- ½ teaspoon paprika
- 1 teaspoon curry powder
- Juice of 1 lemon and 1 lime
- Salt and pepper to taste

Combine diced mango, red pepper, onion, chive, jicama, black beans, honey, ginger, paprika and curry. Add lemon and lime juice. Adjust seasoning with salt and pepper. Refrigerate until served. Keeps well for 4 days in refrigerator.

Makes 4 to 5 cups.

Warm Spinach Salad With Sherry Vinaigrette

- 8 ounces baby leaf spinach, washed and patted dry
- 4 ounces fresh white mushrooms
- 2 tablespoons pancetta (rolled Italian bacon)
- 4 ounces Sherry Vinaigrette (recipe follows)

Heat mushrooms, bacon and Sherry Vinaigrette until hot.

Pour over spinach and toss lightly until all spinach leaves are well coated.

Sherry Vinaigrette

- 2 large egg yolks
- 2 ounces (Dijon mustard)
- 2 cups light salad oil
- 2 ounces sherry vinegar
- Salt and pepper to taste

In mixing bowl with balloon whisk, whip egg yolks and mustard together about 5 minutes. Gradually add salad oil in a thin, steady stream, allowing oil to be incorporated before adding more rapidly. Thin mixture from time to time with sherry vinegar. (Can also make in electric blender.) Adjust seasoning with salt and pepper.

Serves 4.

Grilled Chicken Caesar Salad

- 1¼ pounds boneless chicken breast, grilled
- 2 heads romaine lettuce, torn in ¾-inch pieces
- 2 ounces freshly grated Parmesan cheese
- 4 ounces Monterey Jack cheese
- 4 ounces garlic croutons
- Caesar Dressing (recipe follows)
- 18 red onion rings

Grill chicken breast and slice into thin strips. Wash romaine and pat dry. Toss romaine with cheese, croutons and dressing. Mound on plate and place chicken strips around salad. Chicken can be chilled or at room temperature. Top with onion rings.

Serves 6.

Caesar Dressing

- 2 egg yolks
- 2 ounces Dijon mustard
- 2 cups salad oil
- 2 ounces red wine vinegar
- 1 teaspoon chopped anchovies
- 1 tablespoon finely chopped garlic
- Salt and pepper as needed

In a mixing bowl with a balloon wire whip, whip yolks and mustard about 5 minutes, until combined well.

Slowly add oil, allowing it to be absorbed completely before adding more rapidly.

Thin mixture from time to time with red wine vinegar, adding about 2 ounces each time until all the oil has been used. Add anchovies and garlic. Season as needed with salt and pepper.

Remington on Post Oak Park
1919 Briar Oaks Lane at San Felipe
Houston, Texas 77027
840-7600

Rudi Lechner's

> ## FAVORITES
>
> *White Wine Cheese Soup*
> *Crepe Hubert*
> *Chicken Breast Southern California*
> *Calf Liver With Red Onion-Apple Butter Sauce*
> *Zucchini Nut Bread*

Rudi Lechner just can't stay out of the kitchen. He embarked on a hotel and restaurant career at an early age—he began at 14 as an apprentice in a pastry shop in Austria and was food and beverage manager of a major Washington, D.C., hotel at 24.

He worked for the largest restaurant chain in Europe, Movenpick, before he came to the U.S. in 1964 and ended up in Washington where he helped orchestrate events attended by five U.S. presidents.

"The most eventful thing in my life was taking care of the suite at the Hilton after President Eisenhower died. Mrs. Eisenhower was staying in the hotel and all the leaders came to pay courtesy calls. I opened the door one day and there stood Charles DeGaulle."

Lechner seemed destined for a career in hotel management. He came to Houston in 1973 as food and beverage director of the new Hyatt Regency. But after two years he decided that what he really wanted to do was get back to the kitchen and cook, and he opened La Quiche in 1975. The restaurant helped introduce the trendy dish of the '70s to Houston.

Through the years, La Quiche has segued into a Continental restaurant with a sidewalk cafe ambiance, a European ethnic restaurant and a casual brasserie.

Many of the trendy items on early menus are now classics—quiche, pasta salads, zucchini bread, crepes, fruit soups, cheese soup and steamed baby vegetables.

Lechner has always featured some of his European heritage dishes—strudel, Hungarian goulash, sausages and sauerbraten. Now he's introducing Heritage Cooking, cross-cultural country cooking which mixes European and American heritage dishes.

You find there is a marked kinship between Texas chicken fried steak and Austria's wienerschnitzel; both are pan-fried breaded cutlets. But in Lechner's version of the Texas classic, the steak is stuffed with cheese and jalapenos (on request), deep-fried, then finished in the oven to remove the grease. It is served with a cheese sauce instead of the ubiquitous cream gravy.

Chicken Breast California is only a few generations removed from Chicken Cordon Bleu.

The simplest dishes are the mark of cooking skill, and a simple, but impeccably prepared, roast chicken is one of the most popular specials. The chicken noodle soup is an award-winner.

Some menu items remain constant, but Lechner has so many repeat customers (some dine there several times a week) that he cooks a lot to order and is always adding new selections.

Star Attractions

★ "Heritage" country cooking from a variety of countries, particularly Germany, Austria and America. One of the few restaurants in Houston to feature European ethnic specialties such as roast pork shank, wienerschnitzel, sauerbraten.

★ One of the city's first, and still one of the city's best, salad bars. Specialties include Liptauer cheese, herring salad with red beets and apples, shrimp pate, chicken liver pate, pasta salads, excellent cheese and zucchini breads and soups.

★ All fresh foods and ingredients.

★ Catering for parties from 10 to 200.

★ Wine room which accommodates as many as 20.

★ Comfortable bar with food service.

★ Office delivery within a three-mile radius—$15 or 15 percent delivery charge, whichever is the greater.

★ Take-out menu

★ Casual relaxed neighborhood atmosphere and decor. Dining room is centered by a raised gazebo dining level with dark latticework; wall murals, flower boxes, paintings by an Austrian artist, Tiffany-style hanging lamps, hanging plant baskets.

★ Daily specials; at least two featured nightly at dinner.

★ Breakfast served Monday through Saturday featuring country sausage and biscuits, home fries, Belgian waffles and the Texas Rancher Breakfast—pancakes, sausage and eggs.

★ Annual birthday party in October. Donations go to different charities.

★ Live music series on Saturday night once a month. Features pianist, opera, popular singers.

White Wine Cheese Soup

3	ounces (6 tablespoons) butter
½	cup flour
2	cups chicken stock
1	cup white wine
4	garlic cloves, finely chopped
1½	cups shredded swiss cheese (Emmenthaler)
1	teaspoon chicken seasoned stock base or instant bouillon
1	cup heavy (whipping) cream
2	tablespoons freshly grated Parmesan cheese
½	cup garlic croutons

Melt butter in small pot. Whisk in flour to make a light roux.

Whisk in cold chicken stock, wine and garlic. Let simmer 5 to 10 minutes while stirring with a whisk. Add cheese, chicken base, salt and white pepper to taste. Stir in cream.

Serve in hot soup bowls. Top with Parmesan, croutons and parsley.

Serves 4.

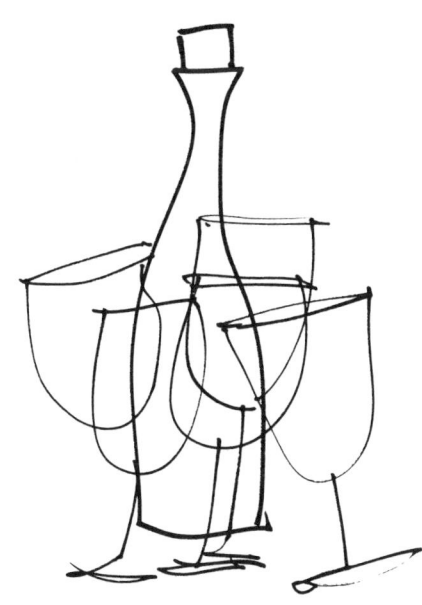

Crepe Hubert

Filling
- 2 tablespoons herb butter
- 2 tablespoons finely chopped onion
- 12 ounces (2 large) boneless, skinless chicken breasts, cut in bite-size pieces
- 12 medium mushrooms, cut in halves
- ⅓ cup chicken stock
- ⅓ cup white wine
- 1 teaspoon chopped fresh parsley
- 1 teaspoon chicken seasoned stock base or instant bouillon
- 2 tablespoons roux
- ½ cup whipping cream
- Crepe Batter (recipe follows)
- Roux (recipe follows)

Heat skillet. Add herb butter and saute onion lightly. Add chicken breast and mushrooms. Saute chicken until it is almost cooked.

Add stock, wine, parsley and chicken base. Bring to a simmer. Whisk in as much cold roux as needed. Finish by whisking in the cream, salt and white pepper to taste.

Reduce heat and stir constantly until thickened and smooth. Place ¼ cup filling in each of 8 crepes. Roll crepes up and top with leftover filling. Place on hot plates and serve with fresh, colorful garden vegetables and rice pilaf.

Serves 4.

Crepe Batter
- ½ cup milk
- ½ cup heavy (whipping) cream
- 1 egg plus 1 egg yolk
- 1¾ cups all-purpose flour
- Salt

Combine milk, cream, eggs and dash of salt in mixing bowl. Whisk in flour (batter should be thin).

Heat crepe pan with 1 teaspoon butter. Pour in about 2 tablespoons crepe batter and turn pan so it covers the bottom (it should be thin). Cook until lightly set. Turn with spatula and cook a few seconds on other side.

Roux
- 1 tablespoon butter
- 2 tablespoons flour

Melt butter in skillet. Stir in flour and whisk until thickened. Do not let brown. Set aside until needed.

Chicken Breast Southern California

- 4 (8-ounce) boneless, skinless chicken breasts
- 5 cloves garlic, finely chopped
- 2 tablespoons bottled teriyaki sauce
- 2 tablespoons honey
- White pepper and salt
- 4 tablespoons olive oil
- 1 each red and green bell peppers, julienned
- 1 onion, chopped

Mix 3 garlic cloves, teriyaki, honey and white pepper to taste. Pound chicken breast lightly. Brush with the mixture. Cover with plastic wrap or place in a plastic bag and chill 2 hours or overnight.

Heat skillet, add olive oil, heat and saute chicken quickly over high heat. Reduce heat gradually until finished. Do not overcook.

Remove chicken from skillet and keep warm. Saute peppers, onion and remaining garlic in the same skillet; peppers should remain crisp-tender. Season to taste with salt and pepper.

Place chicken on serving plate and top with sauteed peppers and onions. Serve with fresh vegetables and potatoes.

Serves 4.

Calf Liver With Red Onion-Apple Butter Sauce

- 4 (6-ounce) slices calf liver
- Flour
- 2 apples
- 4 tablespoons butter
- 2 tablespoons sugar
- 2 medium-size red onions, sliced ¼-inch thick
- 1 cup red Burgundy wine
- 1 teaspoon Worcestershire sauce
- 1 tablespoon brown sugar
- ½ teaspoon black pepper
- ½ teaspoon crushed basil
- ½ teaspoon crushed thyme
- Salt as needed

Peel apples and slice ¼-inch thick. Heat 2 tablespoons butter in skillet. Melt sugar very lightly; do not let brown. Add apples and saute 2 minutes. Remove from heat.

At the same time, in another skillet, saute onion, sliced ¼-inch thick, in 2 tablespoons butter until light gold. Add wine and Worcestershire and simmer over reduced heat.

Combine apples and onions. Add brown sugar and spices. Reduce heat to very low and whisk sauce (it should not be runny). Pepper the liver and dip in flour. Pan-fry in skillet so it remains pink. Do not overcook.

Place liver on serving plate and top with the onion-apple butter sauce. Serve with steamed fresh vegetables and rice pilaf.

Serves 4.

Zucchini Nut Bread

- 4 eggs
- ⅓ cup milk
- 1½ cups sugar
- 3 cups all-purpose flour
- 1 cup vegetable oil
- 1 teaspoon salt
- 1 teaspoon vanilla
- 1 teaspoon lemon juice
- 1½ tablespoons cinnamon
- 2 teaspoons baking powder
- 1 teaspoon soda
- ⅓ cup raisins
- ⅓ cup chopped walnuts
- 1½ cup shredded zucchini

Preheat oven to 350 degrees. Blend 1 egg, milk and 1 teaspoon sugar as an egg wash. Combine flour, oil, salt, vanilla, lemon juice, cinnamon, baking powder, soda, raisins, walnuts and zucchini in food processor and blend, pulsing off and on, until mixed 5 minutes or less.

Fill 2 (9-inch) lightly greased and floured layer cake pans and bake at 350 degrees 30 minutes. Brush with egg wash. Bake 2 more minutes. Serve warm cut in wedges.

Also may be baked in disposable aluminum pie pans.

Rudi Lechner's
2503 S. Gessner
Houston, Texas 77063
782-1180

Thai Cafe

> **FAVORITES**
>
> *Nam Sodd*
> *(Ground Pork Appetizer)*
> *Thai Satay With Cucumber Salad*
> *Thom Ka Gai*
> *(Coconut Chicken Soup)*
> *Papaya Salad*
> *Beef With Sweet Basil*
> *Stir-Fried Vegetables*
> *Sticky Rice and Mango*
> *Thai Tea*

Thai food is a study in intriguing contrasts—hot and cool, spicy and sweet, crunchy and smooth. It fills the mouth with flavors and appeals to all the senses.

One of the early Thai restaurants in Houston, the Thai Cafe has done much to educate Houston to this fascinating cuisine. Anyone who appreciates Chinese, Indian, Vietnamese and even Tex-Mex foods will find Thai appealing.

Although the tastes are entirely different, these worldly cuisines have many ingredients in common including rice, hot peppers, limes, cilantro, ginger, lemon grass and other exotic herbs. The basic sauce is nam pla, a fish sauce that is the Thai equivalent of soy sauce.

Thai cuisine is said to be a balance of five flavors—hot, bitter, sour, sweet and salty—and the Thai Cafe expertly practices this style.

Various regional specialties are featured on the menu including clay pot dishes typical of the northern area; seafood and the famous shrimp dish, gapi, from southern Thailand where the Malaysian influence is strong, and Chinese-style dishes from the middle central area.

The restaurant is a family operation run by Tee Bumrungkittikul and his brother Chai. Their sister opened a new restaurant in Bangkok in 1988.

The brothers came to the U.S. about 15 years ago and Tee earned a degree in electronics at the Delahanty Institute in New York. He came to Houston to visit and ended up moving here and attending the University of Houston. He and his brother gained experience in several Houston restaurants before starting the Thai Cafe in 1984.

The approach is classical, but the spiciness and heat of any dish will be adjusted to the diner's taste. Waiters routinely ask which level of spiciness you prefer. Fiery dishes are indicated by two asterisks by the name on the menu.

The decor of the small 60-seat restaurant also is a blend of the traditional—framed Thai silk embroideries, art work and brass, classical dancer dolls in glass cases—and the contemporary—furniture, colors and fabrics. Dusty rose painted walls are a backdrop for coral, turquoise and rose floral fabrics and hunter green accents, including the cloths that underline the glass tops of the tables.

Star Attractions

★ Blend of classical and contemporary Thai specialties representing a wide range of regional cooking. Spiciness and heat adjusted to your taste—from fiery dishes that will bring tears to your eyes to those that are mild or leave only a warm blush in the mouth.

★ House specialties such as Shrimp Clay Pot, Lob (minced chicken or meat with red and green onion, lime, mint and pepper), Pattaya Fish (deep-fried whole fish with a special ginger sauce), Mee Krob (crispy noodles with pork, onion and garlic in a sweet red sauce), curries and spring rolls.

★ Vegetarian dishes such as stir-fried mixed vegetables, curry, vegetable clay pot and bean curd with ginger.

★ Full service bar. Thai beer when available.

★ Well thought out wine list; strong in California selections. House wines are Simi Cabernet from California, Gekkeikan plum wine from Japan and Chantovent from France. Especially good with spicy foods: Buehler white Zinfandel, Alexander Valley Gewurztraminer and Piesporter Goldtropchen.

★ Will do cooking parties in homes for regular customers.
★ Take-out of most menu items; delivery service within a two-mile radius of restaurant.
★ Catering available.
★ Open seven days a week for dinner; open Saturday night until midnight; lunch Monday through Friday.

Nam Sodd (Ground Pork Appetizer)

- ½ pound ground pork
- 3 ounces shredded pork skin*
- 1 tablespoon roasted peanuts
- 1 tablespoon each chopped red and green onion
- 1½ teaspoons lime juice
- ½ teaspoon bottled fish sauce (nam pla)
  Shredded fresh ginger to taste
- ¼ teaspoon dried red pepper
- ½ teaspoon paprika
- ½ teaspoon sugar
- 6 to 8 cucumber slices
  Green beans (raw or quickly blanched, but not cooked)

*Shredded pork skins are the Thai equivalent of cracklings; they are found in 4-ounce plastic packages in the freezer section of Oriental food import shops; Golden Dragon is one brand Bumrungkittikul recommends.

Place ground pork and shredded pork skin in saucepan, cover with water and bring to a boil. Boil until pork is completely cooked and has lost all its pink color. Drain thoroughly.

Mix in peanuts, onion, lime juice, fish sauce, ginger, red pepper, paprika and sugar. Line an oval plate with leaf lettuce and arrange pork on top extending out from lettuce. Garnish with cucumber and raw green beans. This is extremely hot, but delicious; you may want to cut back on the red pepper and ginger.

Serves 1.

Satay With Peanut Butter Sauce and Cucumber Salad

- 1 pound flank steak, pork or chicken, sliced in thin 3x¾-inch strips
- ½ cup coconut milk (not cream of coconut)
- 2½ ounces curry powder (gang ga-lee)
  Dash of salt
- ½ cup milk
- ¼ teaspoon turmeric
  Peanut Butter Sauce (recipe follows)
  Cucumber Salad (recipe follows)

Combine meat slices, coconut milk, curry powder, salt, milk and turmeric; marinate at least 10 hours in the refrigerator. Char-grill and serve with sauce for dipping.

Peanut Butter Sauce
- 1 ounce Thai red curry paste (Gang Dang)
- ¼ cup coconut milk
- 2 tablespoons chunky peanut butter
- 1 teaspoon sugar
- 1 teaspoon Thai fish sauce (nam pla)

Mix curry paste with coconut milk and saute over low heat 2 minutes in saucepan. Add peanut butter, sugar and fish sauce and cook another 3 to 5 minutes. Store in refrigerator and reheat in the microwave about 1 minute before serving.

This is traditionally served with satay, but is a wonderful condiment with other dishes such as Oriental chicken salads.

Cucumber Salad
- ¼ sweet red onion, cut in small strips
- 1 cucumber, peeled, thinly sliced and quartered
- ¼ cup white vinegar
- 1 teaspoon light corn syrup or sugar

Combine onion, cucumber, vinegar and syrup. If using sugar, be sure it is completely dissolved. Serve with satay or as a relish with other appetizers or green salad.

Coconut Chicken Soup (Thom Ka Gai)

- 10 ounces coconut milk (not cream of coconut)
- 1 cup chicken broth
- 4 ounces chicken, sliced in thin 1-inch long strips
- 2 ounces canned straw mushrooms or fresh mushrooms (about 8 per person)
- 1½ teaspoons fish sauce (nam pla)
- ½ ounce (about 4 slices) galangal or Siamese ginger (ka)
- 1 ounce lemon grass, cut in 1-inch pieces
- 2 teaspoons lime juice
- 4 lemon leaves (bai makrut)
- 1 tablespoon shrimp curry paste (nam prik paw)
- 1 serrano pepper, sliced
- Cilantro for garnish

Combine coconut milk and broth in saucepan and cook over medium heat until boiling. Add chicken, mushrooms, nam pla, ginger, lemon grass, lime juice and lemon leaves; boil until chicken is cooked, about 3 to 5 minutes.

Mix shrimp curry paste with serrano; spoon into bowl. Pour soup over it and garnish with cilantro.

At Thai Cafe, the dish also is garnished with fanciful flowers carved from hot peppers or other vegetables.

Serves 4 to 6.

Papaya Salad

- 1 cup shredded green papaya
- 1 clove garlic
- 1 teaspoon crushed roasted peanuts
- 1 Thai chile
- 3 green beans, cut into 1 inch pieces
- 1 teaspoon fresh lime juice
- ½ teaspoon bottled fish sauce (nam pla)
- ½ teaspoon sugar
- 3 cherry tomatoes
- 2 to 3 leaves leaf lettuce

Peel and slice papaya lengthwise. With knife, slice or cut in julienne strips.

Crush garlic, peanut and chile very fine with mortar and pestle (handle chile carefully and avoid getting it on hands, in eyes or breathing fumes).

Mix in papaya, green beans, lime juice, fish sauce and sugar. Wrap a spoonful of mixture in small piece of leaf lettuce and roll up or fold to make bite-size pieces. Garnish plate with cherry tomatoes.

Serves 1.

Beef With Sweet Basil

- 10 ounces thinly sliced boneless beef sirloin or tenderloin
- ½ cup chopped white onion
- ½ cup chopped bell pepper
- 2 serrano peppers, sliced
- 2 tablespoons cooking oil
- 6 to 8 sweet basil leaves
- 1 tablespoon sweet soy sauce
- 1 teaspoon fish sauce (nam pla) or salt
- ½ cup chicken broth

Saute beef slices with onion, bell pepper and serranos in oil over high heat until beef is cooked. Add basil, soy sauce, fish sauce and broth and cook 1 more minute. Serve on plate with plain steamed rice.

Serves 1.

Sticky Rice and Mango

For some, this sweet, glutinous rice is an acquired taste, but if you like it, you really like it.

- 2 cups raw sticky rice (glutinous sweet rice)
- 1½ cups coconut milk (not cream of coconut)
- ¾ cup sugar syrup
  Pinch of salt
- 2 to 3 large fresh mangos

Soak rice at least 4 hours or overnight. Place a piece of dampened cotton cloth or cheesecloth on rack in Oriental steamer basket and place rice on cheesecloth. Or use double boiler with steamer insert. Cook rice over simmering, not boiling, water (you can use water in which rice was soaked). Rice should not touch water. Steam covered until cooked, about 20 minutes.

Heat coconut milk to a simmer. Stir in sugar syrup and salt. Continue simmering 3 minutes. Combine rice with enough of the coconut milk mixture to make it creamy. Allow to cool and let sit at room temperature about 1 hour to absorb coconut milk and thicken. It shouldn't be soupy; you may have some coconut milk mixture left over.

Form portions of rice into 8 balls about 3 inches in diameter. Peel and slice mangos. Place one mound of rice on a plate, flatten slightly and top with a few slices of mango. Garnish with more mango, a strawberry or other fresh fruit.

Serves 8.

Notes: If desired, microwave sugar syrup in 1-quart glass measure on high until thickened and syrupy, 4 to 5 minutes; watch carefully and do not let boil over. Warm coconut milk in microwave container, add sugar syrup and microwave 1 to 2 minutes on medium-high; stir well with whisk.

Rice balls may be made up ahead of time and stored in freezer. Wrap each in plastic wrap and freeze in a plastic freezer bag. When ready to use, microwave each on high for about 1 minute to thaw.

Some Thai cooks substitute canned cream of coconut for coconut milk and omit the sugar syrup.

Stir-Fried Vegetables

- 2½ cups mixed fresh vegetables (broccoli florets, bell pepper chunks or slices, chopped onion, snow peas, bamboo shoots, sliced mushrooms)
- 2 tablespoons cooking oil
- 3 tablespoons bottled oyster sauce
- 1 teaspoon sugar
- ¼ cup chicken broth

Heat oil in wok or skillet. Add vegetables and stir-fry over high heat 1 minute. Add oyster sauce, sugar and broth.

Stir-fry over high heat 2 more minutes; vegetables should remain crisp-tender. Serve with steamed or fried rice.

Serves 1.

Thai Tea

- 8 cups boiling water
- 1¼ cups loose Thai tea
- 1½ cups sugar
  Evaporated milk

Bring water to a boil, add tea and brew until very dark. Strain through a coffee filter. Discard tea leaves. Add sugar to tea; stir until dissolved. Keep in refrigerator. To serve: Pour tea into tall glasses over ice; stir in milk as desired.

Serves 4.

Diet Alert: Can sweeten tea to taste with sugar substitute.

Thai Cafe
10928 Westheimer at Lakeside Estates
Houston, Texas 77042
780-3096

Tony's

FAVORITES

Swordfish Salad
Eggplant Terrine
Poussin (Baby Chicken) Framboise
Breast of Chicken With Peppercorn
Braciole alla Napoletana
Apple Tart Tony's

If there were only one restaurant that set Houston on the path to epicurean dining, it would be Tony's. The elegant restaurant in the Galleria area provides a feast for all the senses, and has been recognized in the U.S. and internationally by food critics, celebrities and food and wine connoisseurs.

As the best people-watching spot in town, Tony's is a social event itself, but fine foodstuffs and great wines are the setpiece of the namesake of gifted restaurateur Tony Vallone.

Under the direction of Vallone and executive chef Mark Cox, a graduate of the Culinary Institute of America, the cuisine is a blend of European tradition and American improvisation.

Guests at Tony's quickly sense the dedication of the owner, general manager Tino Escobedo, the chef and staff. To enter you pass displays of rare wines and the gastronomic treasures of the season. A custom-designed glass and wood cabinet displays the rarest of wines from a collection of more than 60,000 bottles and has its own refrigeration and security alarm. Among the gems: a 1795 Madeira (a gift from a loyal customer), a rare 1844 Chateau Lafite-Rothschild and an 1811 Vieux Cognac.

On rounded tiered shelves at the entrance to the dining room are still lifes of real food—thumb-sized fresh blackberries or golden raspberries from Oregon, white truffles from Italy, samples of special dishes from the menu, fat jars of olives, cheeses (perhaps flown in from New York or Europe); magnums of wine and Champagne, olive oil (including Tony's current favorite Nevi), and tins of caviar in silver compotes.

Everywhere there are fresh flowers; a towering arrangement even tops the dessert cart. A measure of Tony Vallone's attention to detail is that he employs an in-house florist.

The flowers, fabrics and collection of Chinese porcelains are a visual extension of the colors in the modern paintings that line the claret walls. Turquoise, blues, coral, luminous gold and rose are drawn from the priceless twenty-six-foot Chinese watercolor screen (circa 1690) that dominates one long wall.

Tony's menu has evolved through Italian to Continental to French to simply "the poetry of dining" since he opened at the present location in 1972, but one tenet has remained constant—obtain the finest, freshest ingredients and treat them with respect.

Star Attractions

★ Polished orchestration of all the elements of fine dining—food, wine, service, ambiance.

★ Innovative cuisine with classic foundation. Tony Vallone seeks out the finest ingredients from all over the world—cheeses, porcini mushrooms and white truffles, fish, olive oils, vinegars. Some specialty items are grown locally such as pepperoncini and poblano peppers and ruffled opal basil.

Sauces are light and silky, never overpowering. Fish, meats and chicken are grilled with care. Dessert souffles rise to impressive heights.

A current success is an appetizer of sauteed zucchini squash blossoms with a stuffing of lobster and Fontina cheese with a chive butter sauce.

★ Recipes for many of the restaurant specialties are included in "Tony's—The Cookbook" (published by Shearer in 1986).

★ Caters to customers' requests from chili and chicken fried steak to modifying dishes to fit the Pritikin diet.

★ The Bordeaux Room and wine cellar are available for special dinners and parties. Baccarat and Val St. Lambert crystal; Royal Doulton china.

★ "The" place to see and be seen and to celebrate life's memorable events such as birthdays, engagements and wedding anniversaries.

★ National and international recognition. Tony's has earned the Mobil Four Star restaurant award for 15 years and Travel Holiday Award for 17 years. Tony Vallone is the first American-born member of the prestigious Gruppi Ristoratori Italiani dedicated to the improvement of appreciation of Italian food around the world and is a member of the strictly Italian group Ciao Italia.

★ Tony's is a frequent setting for dinners given by such gourmet dining societies as the International Wine and Food Society and the Confrerie de la Chaine des Rotisseurs.

★ One of the nation's best wine lists.

★ Involvement in civic and social affairs such as the March of Dimes Gourmet Gala and Cystic Fibrosis benefits. Donates food to the End Hunger Loop project of the End Hunger Network.

Swordfish Salad

- 1 cup torn romaine
- 1 cup torn arugula
- 2 each: broccoli florets and cauliflower florets
  About 1 cup julienned vegetables: carrots, celery and red bell pepper
  Mushrooms and sweet red pepper strips for garnish
- ½ pound swordfish fillet, grilled
  Honey Mustard Dressing (recipe follows)

Combine romaine, arugula, broccoli and cauliflower florets and julienned vegetables. Toss well with the honey mustard dressing, garnish with mushrooms and sweet red peppers.

Grill swordfish lightly; it should remain undercooked. Slice thinly and arrange it on the salad. Garnish as desired with mushrooms and peppers.

Honey Mustard Dressing
Combine 1 tablespoon light vegetable oil and 3 tablespoons red wine vinegar; add Dijon mustard and honey to taste.

Serves 1.

Eggplant Terrine

- ½ cup oil-packed sun-dried tomatoes, drained
- 1 bunch fresh basil (about ½ cup leaves)
- 2 cups chicken stock
- 3 medium eggplants, peeled and sliced lengthwise ⅛-inch thick
- ¾ cup extra-virgin olive oil
- 1 pound shiitake mushrooms, stems removed, chopped
- 6 shallots and 3 garlic cloves, chopped together
  Salt and pepper to taste
- 4 large red bell peppers, roasted, peeled and seeded

Preheat oven to 350 degrees. Puree tomatoes with basil leaves and ⅓ cup stock; set aside.

Square off eggplant slices to fit a 1-quart loaf pan and place on a Teflon sheet. Season to taste and brush eggplant with oil, using all but 6 tablespoons. Bake at 350 degrees until evenly browned, 20 to 25 minutes.

Heat remaining oil in a pan, and saute mushrooms in small batches until crisp; drain on paper towels.

Saute shallot mixture until transparent; drain. Return mushrooms and shallots to pan, add remaining stock and cook over high heat until liquid evaporates. Puree, season to taste with salt and pepper and set aside.

Cut each pepper into 4 segments; pound flat between layers of plastic wrap.

Oil a loaf pan. To assemble: Place a layer of 2 to 3 eggplant slices in bottom of pan; top with a layer of red peppers (4 pieces), another layer of eggplant, mushrooms, layer of eggplant, layer of tomato mixture and a final layer of eggplant.

Cover terrine with foil, place in a larger pan, add hot water to come half way up on the terrine and bake 1 hour 15 minutes at 350 degrees. Remove terrine from water bath and let cool.

Place a weight on top of foil. Refrigerate 12 hours. To serve, cut in slices. Serve as an appetizer or a vegetable accompaniment or plate garnish for chicken, meats or seafood.

Serves 8.

Poussin Framboise

- 2 poussin (baby chickens—1¼ pounds), squab, Cornish hens or favorite small bird cut in half lengthwise
- 3 cups fresh raspberries or blackberries
- ½ pound butter
- Seasoned salt and freshly ground pepper
- 2 tablespoons extra-virgin Italian olive oil
- 1 teaspoon framboise liqueur
- 1 tablespoon sugar

Slit the birds down the back, cut out the backbone, flatten the sides and fold the wings under. Reserve 24 raspberries for garnish. Press the rest through a sieve. Divide berries in half.

Mix half the berries in a food processor with the butter, salt, pepper and framboise. Add the other half to the processor with the sugar and 2 tablespoons olive oil.

Season the birds well and cover all over with oil and puree mixture. Let marinate 1 hour at room temperature.

Start a charcoal fire or preheat the broiler. Grill the birds, breast side down, 8 minutes, turning them so they cook and mark evenly. Finish cooking, cavity side down, for about another 8 or 10 minutes until golden brown (do not overcook).

Serve half a chicken per person. Garnish each with 6 raspberries and spoon some of the raspberry-butter mixture over each. Serve with fresh julienned vegetables.

Breast of Chicken With Peppercorns

- 1½ ounces clarified butter
- 7 ounces boneless chicken breast, cut into 1-ounce medallions
- ¼ teaspoon each salt and black pepper
- 1 tablespoon finely chopped shallots
- 1 tablespoon each diced red and yellow bell peppers
- 2 teaspoons crushed green peppercorns
- 1½ ounces Jameson Irish Whiskey
- ¼ cup chicken stock
- 3 tablespoons heavy (whipping) cream
- ½ tablespoon (1½ teaspoons) finely diced sun-dried tomato
- ½ tablespoon finely diced black olives

Heat skillet, then add and heat clarified butter. Season chicken breast with salt and pepper. Saute chicken 4 minutes on each side. Remove and reserve.

Add shallots, stirring until transparent. Add peppers, peppercorns and whiskey. Flambe by carefully lighting with a taper match. Add chicken stock and bring to a simmer. Stir in cream. Adjust seasoning.

Spoon sauce onto plate. Arrange chicken breast on top. Sprinkle with sun-dried tomato and black olives.

Serves 1.

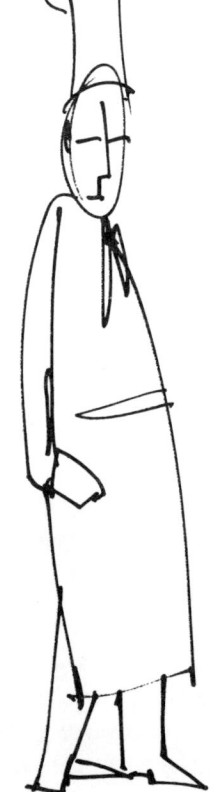

Braciole alla Napoletana

- ⅓ cup raisins
- ¼ pound prosciutto or Italian salami, finely chopped
- ⅓ fresh bread crumbs
- ⅓ cup pine nuts
- ⅓ cup minced fresh parsley
- ¾ cup freshly grated Parmesan cheese
- ½ teaspoon seasoned salt
- 1 teaspoon freshly ground pepper
- 1½ pounds beef top round, cut into 3 pieces about ¼-inch thick
- ⅓ cup extra-virgin Italian olive oil
- 1 small red onion, chopped
- 1 small carrot, chopped
- ½ cup dry red wine
- 1 (32-ounce) can Italian San Marzano tomatoes chopped, juice reserved

In a medium bowl, combine the raisins, prosciutto, bread crumbs, pine nuts, parsley, Parmesan and half each of the salt and pepper. Mix well and set aside.

Cut each beef slice into thirds to form nine pieces about 3½x3 inches. Divide the filling evenly among the meat slices and spread to cover, leaving ¼ inch around the edge.

Roll the slices into rounds, tuck in the ends if possible and secure with toothpicks.

In a large pan or casserole, heat the olive oil, add the onion and carrot and cook over moderate heat until the onion is translucent, about 3 to 5 minutes.

Remove vegetables from pan and set aside. Add the meat rolls to the pan, seam side down. Increase the heat and saute until meat is browned on all sides. Remove meat and set aside.

Add the wine to the pan and bring to a boil, scraping up any browned meat bits. Boil 1 minute. Reduce the heat. Return meat and vegetables to the pan, add the tomato juice and tomatoes. Season with salt and pepper.

Simmer covered over low heat until the meat is tender, about 1½ hours. Remove toothpicks, skim off any fat and serve with sauce poured over it.

Serves 6 to 8.

Note: If a thicker sauce is desired, add a tablespoon of tomato paste and a teaspoon of sugar and let simmer about 15 minutes. If too thick, thin with stock.

Apple Tart

Crust
- 1½ cups all-purpose flour
- 4 ounces (½ cup) very cold unsalted butter, cut in small pieces
- ¾ teaspoon sugar
- ⅛ teaspoon salt
- ¼ cup (about) cold water

Mix flour with butter, sugar and salt. (Use hands to mix butter into flour.) When finished, small bits of butter should still be visible in the dough. Add water and continue kneading until ingredients hold together. Refrigerate.

Filling
- 3½ pounds cooking apples such as Granny Smiths
- 1 cup sugar
- ½ cup unsalted butter
- 1 cup water

Roll out dough, cut out a 9-inch circle and place on a cookie sheet. Puncture dough all over with a fork. Bake unfilled in a 400-degree oven 10 minutes. Cool. Slide onto serving plate.

Peel, core and slice apples. Mix sugar, butter and water in a heavy skillet and cook until syrup is formed. Saute apples in syrup 5 to 6 minutes.

When soft, pour onto large cookie sheet to cool. When cool, arrange slices on tart shell. Cover with the remaining caramel syrup. Serve immediately.

Serves 8.

Tony's
1801 Post Oak Boulevard
Houston, Texas 77056
622-6778

Tony Mandola's

The North Shepherd restaurant, which is moving to the River Oaks Shopping Center, is scheduled to open in the early fall of '88. Both the River Oaks and Gulf Freeway restaurants are casual, comfortable settings in which to enjoy home-style foods with a personal flair.

FAVORITES

Ceviche
Shrimp Cocktail Vicente
Deviled Crab/Crab Balls
Red Beans and Rice With Sausage
Seafood Lasagna
Tony Mandola's Bread Puddin' With Whiskey Sauce

Star Attractions

★ Casual, relaxed restaurant with New Orleans flavor and home-style food.

★ Fresh seafood handled in ingenious ways. The Shrimp Cocktail Vicente, named for owner Tony Mandola's brother Vincent, combines Italian and Tex-Mex flavors. Served as an appetizer, the shrimp is layered in a sundae glass with pico de gallo, cocktail sauce, avocado and lime wedges.

For nachos, Mandola suggests that guests spoon some of the mixture onto freshly made tortilla chips; the nachos make a great party appetizer, he says. Mandola turns the strained broth in which the shrimp was cooked into a tortilla soup by adding fried tortilla strips.

Deviled crab is prepared as a casserole, but the mixture also can be served in crab shells or rolled into balls and fried as an appetizer.

For Oysters Damian, named for Mandola's other brother, oysters are fried, put back on the half shell and served with pico de gallo.

★ Catering available.

★ Mama's specials including spaghetti served on Tuesdays and Thursdays.

Tony Mandola's restaurants feature the same type of "good, honest fresh food" that his mother Grace grew up with in Lake Charles, Louisiana, and cooked for her children when they were growing up in Houston.

Then you could almost tell the day of the week by the menu. Friday night was spaghetti night, and Mama usually threw a few shrimp and crab into the sauce. Saturday night she made meatballs, and the kids would have hamburgers from part of the ground beef. Sunday the meatballs went into the spaghetti sauce to serve as an appetizer. Monday was soup day.

Other days, Creole Rice (his mother's version of jambalaya), Dirty Rice, red beans, rice and sausage, fried shrimp and oysters (lightly shaken in cornmeal in a brown bag), and other legendary Creole dishes showed up on the table. Nothing was wasted.

Small wonder that three of Mama Grace's offspring own some of the most successful restaurants in Houston—Damian's, Nino's and Tony Mandola's. Tony is married to the former Phyllis Laurenzo of the Ninfa's restaurant family

92 / HOUSTON GOURMET COOKS 2

Red Beans, Sausage and Rice

- 8 ounces dried red kidney beans
- 1 pound smoked sausage
- Oil (optional)
- 3 ounces salt pork
- 4 ounces yellow onion (1 medium), finely chopped
- 1 rib celery, finely chopped
- ¼ large bell pepper (1½ ounces), finely chopped
- 1½ teaspoons ground cumin (cominos)
- 1 bay leaf
- ½ teaspoon ground black pepper
- ½ teaspoon cayenne pepper
- 8½ ounces crushed whole canned tomatoes (or ½ pound fresh tomatoes, seeded and crushed)
- ¾ ounce chicken seasoned stock base or instant bouillon
- 2 cups water
- 4 medium cloves garlic (¼ ounce), chopped
- 1 to 2 tablespoons chopped fresh parsley
- 8 servings hot cooked rice

Soak beans overnight or use short-soak method: Place dried beans in large pot; cover with water; bring to a boil and let boil 2 minutes. Turn heat off, cover pan and let sit 1 hour.

While beans soak, place sausage in large non-stick skillet, add water to cover, bring to a boil and let simmer until water has evaporated.

Let sausage cook until browned on both sides, adding a little oil if necessary to keep from sticking. Set aside to cool. Cut sausage in half lengthwise, then into 1½-inch pieces; set aside.

Cut salt pork into 1x1½-inch chunks and cook in a frying pan. Set aside.

In large pot, saute onion, celery and bell pepper in sausage drippings or small amount of oil. When they start to soften, add cumin, bay leaf, black pepper and cayenne.

Return beans to pan, add crushed tomatoes and bring to a boil. Add chicken base or bouillon, water, chopped vegetables, salt pork and half its drippings.

Bring to a boil and add sausage. Reduce heat to medium and let simmer 1 to 1½ hours, stirring frequently. If necessary, add more water occasionally to prevent sticking. Remove from heat and stir in garlic and parsley. Serve beans and sausage over rice.

Serves 8.

Diet Alert: Use non-stick pans and as little oil as possible. Substitute turkey sausage for regular sausage and chunks of lean ham for salt pork.

Shrimp Cocktail Vicente

- 1 ounce onion (about 2 tablespoons chopped)
- ½ ounce (1 small) jalapeno, seeded and diced
- 2 tomatoes, seeded and diced
- 2 garlic cloves, pressed
- Vegetable oil
- Salt and ground black pepper
- Water
- 2½ pounds shrimp, cooked and peeled
- Pico de Gallo
- Seafood cocktail sauce
- Avocado wedges
- 1 lime
- Cilantro sprigs

Saute onion, jalapeno, tomatoes and garlic in 1 tablespoon oil in large non-stick skillet or pot. When soft, add enough water to cover shrimp and bring to a boil. Add shrimp and simmer about 5 minutes (or remove pot from heat, cover and let stand 5 to 10 minutes or until shrimp turn pink). Drain shrimp, saving broth (shrimp also may be cooked in packaged shrimp or crab boil). Peel shrimp and chill thoroughly.

To serve as an appetizer, place a few tablespoons pico de gallo in the bottom of a sundae glass. Top with shrimp, a little red seafood cocktail sauce and more pico de gallo. Pour a little of the chilled shrimp broth over top. Garnish with avocado and lime wedges and cilantro sprigs.

Deviled Crab

- 4 ounces (1 stick) butter
- 2 cups chopped onion
- 1½ cups chopped celery
- Salt and pepper
- ½ teaspoon cayenne pepper
- 1½ cloves garlic, diced
- ¾ cup green onion, chopped (with tops)
- ¼ cup chopped fresh parsley
- ½ cup flour
- 2 cups milk
- 2 pounds crab meat, cleaned and picked
- 1 cup plain dry bread crumbs

Heat a large frying pan and melt butter. Add onion and celery and saute about 15 minutes, until softened, but not brown. Add salt, pepper and cayenne.

Add diced garlic, green onion and parsley. Stir in flour and milk. Cook, stirring until thickened, 5 to 8 minutes.

Remove from heat. Add crabmeat and bread crumbs. Mix thoroughly; serve in real or ceramic crab shells.

To serve as a casserole, turn mixture into a shallow 3-quart casserole, top with dry bread crumbs, dot with butter and heat in oven at 325 degrees until heated through. Or microwave on high power about 6 minutes.

Diet Alert: Use non-stick pan, spray with non-stick spray, substitute soft margarine for butter and reduce amount to 2 tablespoons. Use skim milk and omit salt or use salt substitute. Make bread crumbs of toasted diet bread.

To make Crab Balls: Roll portions of mixture into ¾-ounce balls, about 1-inch in diameter. If mixture is too moist, add more dry bread crumbs. Dip crab balls in beaten egg and roll in bread crumbs. Deep-fry to golden brown.

Seafood Lasagna

- 12 ounces lasagna noodles, cooked, drained and set aside in cold water
- 1 tablespoon crushed basil
- 1 tablespoon crushed oregano
- 1 cup spaghetti sauce
- 2 pounds ricotta cheese
- Olive oil
- 1 pound fresh crabmeat
- 1½ pounds shrimp, cooked and peeled
- 1 cup freshly grated Parmesan cheese
- 8 ounces sliced Mozzarella cheese
- Lasagna Sauce (recipe follows)

Add basil, oregano and 1 cup spaghetti sauce to ricotta in mixing bowl; mix well.

Rub olive oil on bottom and sides of a 13x9x2-inch casserole. Place one layer of noodles on bottom and cover with ricotta mixture. Sprinkle crabmeat over ricotta.

Arrange the cooked shrimp on top of crab. Sprinkle with Parmesan and top with a layer of Mozzarella slices and some of the sauce.

Repeat layers, ending with noodles. Cover with Lasagna Sauce, reserving some to serve with lasagna. Cover pan and bake at 350 degrees 45 minutes or until bubbly.

Cut into 9 servings. Serve each topped with Lasagna Sauce.

Lasagna Sauce

- 6 ounces (1½ sticks) butter
- 1 quart heavy (whipping) cream
- 1 teaspoon cayenne pepper (or to taste)
- ½ ounce chopped shallots (about 1 to 2 large)
- 1 cup spaghetti sauce
- 1 cup freshly grated Parmesan cheese

Heat saucepan and melt butter. Whisk in cream, cayenne, chopped shallots and spaghetti sauce and let simmer a few minutes. Whisk in Parmesan and simmer, stirring, until smooth.

Diet Alert: Substitute farmer's cheese or part-skim milk ricotta for ricotta, reduce amount and use part-skim milk Mozzarella in lasagna. Replace butter with soft margarine and substitute light cream, half-and-half or canned evaporated skim milk for whipping cream in sauce. Reduce portion size.

Ceviche

- 1 pound skinless red snapper fillets, diced
- 1 cup fresh lime juice
- 2½ teaspoons salt
- 1½ large tomatoes (12 ounces), diced
- 4 small carrots, diced
- 1½ large onions (1 pound), diced
- 4 fresh jalapenos, seeded and diced (or to taste)
- 3 canned pickled jalapenos, diced (or to taste)
- 1½ cups peeled, diced cooked shrimp (12 ounces)
- 1 teaspoon bottled red pepper sauce
- 1 teaspoon bottled Louisiana hot sauce
- 3 tablespoons chopped cilantro

Pour lime juice over snapper, sprinkle with salt and refrigerate covered overnight.

Next day, dice tomatoes, carrot, onion and jalapeno and combine with pepper sauce, hot sauce, shrimp, snapper and cilantro in a large bowl. Toss lightly to mix well. Garnish with more chopped cilantro if desired. Refrigerate promptly after serving.

Serves 10 as an appetizer.

Tony Mandola's Bread Puddin' With Whiskey Sauce

- ½ loaf white bread, cut or torn in small squares, about 4 cups
- 1½ teaspoons ground cinnamon
- ¾ teaspoon ground nutmeg
- 2 cups milk
- 2 ounces (¼ cup) evaporated milk
- 2 tablespoons butter
- 2 eggs
- ½ cup sugar
- ¾ teaspoon vanilla
- ¼ cup raisins

Add cinnamon and nutmeg to bread and mix. Let mixture sit overnight.

Next day, preheat oven to 375 degrees (350 if using ovenproof glass casserole). Mix milk, evaporated milk and butter and heat until warm and butter is melted, about 2 minutes in the microwave.

Combine eggs, sugar and vanilla in electric blender and process until smooth. Pour milk and egg mixtures over bread. Add raisins and mix well.

Pour into greased shallow 1½-quart casserole and bake at 350 degrees until firm, about 20 to 30 minutes. Or microwave on high 2 minutes, stir thoroughly, turn dish a quarter turn and microwave 8 to 10 more minutes. Cool on counter.

Cut in squares and serve with Whiskey Sauce.

Whiskey Sauce

- 3 egg yolks, beaten
- 3 cups milk
- 1 cup sugar
- 3 tablespoons cornstarch
- 1¾ ounces bourbon

Combine beaten egg yolks, milk, sugar and cornstarch in medium saucepan. Heat slowly to a boil while whisking constantly. Remove from heat and stir in bourbon. Let sauce cool before refrigerating. Chill and serve over bread pudding. Makes about 1 quart.

Diet Alert: Use skim milk and subsitute egg whites for part of the whole eggs. Use 1 egg and 3 egg whites in bread pudding mixture and egg substitute or 2 egg yolks plus 3 egg whites in Whiskey Sauce.

Tony Mandola's
8105 Gulf Freeway
Houston, Texas 77017
640-1117

Tony Mandola's
River Oaks Shopping Center on West Gray
Houston, Texas 77007
864-0915

Vargo's

FAVORITES

Cheese Spread
Shrimp Scampi
Veal Scallopini al Marsala
Vargo's Special Filet
Chicken alla Romana
Chocolate Roll

In its park-like setting with moss-hung trees, flower gardens, swans gliding across the lake and peacocks strutting over the grounds, Vargo's is like the permanent set for a romantic movie.

A Houston institution for almost a quarter of a century, it has been the scene of countless weddings (about three or four a week during the wedding "season") as well as memorable times-of-our-lives events. Three generations of some families have had dinner at Vargo's before senior proms, and it is "the" place to get engaged, celebrate anniversaries, birthdays and holidays. As many as 1100 have been served on New Year's Eve.

The peacocks fanning their plumage in the parking lot and grounds set the color scheme. After a recent redecoration, the dining room in cool, rich peacock blues and greens seems just an extension of the outdoors. The changing seasons and weather make Vargo's a visual feast, especially during rain storms, during azalea season or at Christmas time when the trees sparkle with 25,000 twinkle lights.

Owner Al Vargo found the property 34 years ago when Westheimer was a quiet two-lane street, but he was not able to talk the owner into selling him a few acres until 24 years ago. The property includes Lake Vargo, which has been there more than 100 years.

One historical anecdote, which Vargo has not been able to substantiate, is that at one time it was called Sam Houston Artesian Springs because Houston camped three days in the area while planning the battle of San Jacinto.

Vargo employs three yardmen and a feed man to care for the grounds and the wildlife—thousands of azaleas, camellias and other flowers, swans, ducks, fish, flamingos, about 30 peacocks, squirrels, rabbits, birds and, once, a small alligator.

Muscovy ducks wing in on their way south and north, and Vargo says he caught the biggest bass he ever caught in the lake.

The multi-level chalet-like restaurant offers a variety of dining experiences from the lively cocktail lounge and terrace to the comfortable clubroom wih fireplace and private party room. The main dining room offers restful glimpses of the lake and rolling grounds through a glass window wall shaded by towering trees.

The menu includes favorites that have proved themselves in the past 24 years—a complimentary appetizer tray featuring cheese spread, vegetable relishes and spiced apples, fine beef, chicken, delicious breads and fresh vegetables.

To prepare the fresh green beans daily, two kitchen helpers work full time snapping beans, Vargo said.

The all-time favorite dessert, Chocolate Roll, was added to the menu years ago at the suggestion of a cook, now retired, Margaret Salke. She had made it when she was a baker at the White House during Franklin Roosevelt's presidency and thought it would go over well at Vargo's.

Star Attractions

★ Setting that is a visual feast—multi-level restaurant with a back-to-nature view of Lake Vargo and the beautifully maintained grounds which are home to all kinds of water fowl and other wildlife.

★ Continental cuisine. Emphasis on fish, seafood, chicken and beef; dishes conform to American Heart Association guidelines. As recognition of changing tastes in foods, lighter fare is being offered at lunch.

★ Piano nightly.

★ Use only Certified Angus Beef.

★ Complimentary appetizer tray.

★ Seated Sunday brunch with complimentary champagne and piano music.

★ Popular location for high school prom dinner for more than 20 years. During the prom season, more than 900 students a weekend come to Vargo's for dinner before the prom.

★ Chef Giuseppe Briguglio's specialties including fresh rainbow trout Meuniere, calf liver Berlin, seafood crepes, grilled jumbo Gulf shrimp, Chicken Cordon Bleu.

★ Vargo's "20 Year Tradition"—entrees served family style with a complimentary relish tray, fruit cup or mixed green salad, fresh green beans, Louisiana dirty rice, whipped potatoes, spiced apples, hot French bread and butter.

Traditional entrees include Gulf Shrimp Henry stuffed with crabmeat, Fresh Red Snapper Albert, Roast Long Island Duckling, Double Frenched Lamb Chops and a special fillet.

★ The restaurant has its own credit card, Vargo's Preferred Charge Card.

★ Separate banquet menu available. Restaurant seats 350 and has a variety of dining rooms.

★ Mobil diamond award.

Vargo's Cheese Spread

½ pound margarine or butter
1½ pounds cream cheese, softened
2 tablespoons finely chopped fresh chives
1 tablespoon paprika
 Dash of salt
¼ teaspoon ground white pepper
 2 to 4 ice cubes

Blend margarine, cream cheese, chives, paprika, salt and white pepper in blender or food processor until it rises to the top of the container.

Add ice cubes and process until mixture has a very creamy consistency. Refrigerate 30 to 45 minutes before serving.

Cheese mixture may be molded into a ball after it has been chilled. Garnish as desired.

Diet Alert: Use soft tub margarine and light cream cheese.

Shrimp Scampi

- 36 super jumbo shrimp, cleaned, deveined and butterflied
- Scampi Butter (recipe follows)
- ⅓ cup fresh chopped parsley
- Salt, pepper and paprika

Make Scampi Butter. To butterfly shrimp: Slice through the back to the front, starting ¼ inch from the top of the tail (don't cut all the way through). Pull the tail under the front through the slit and press the sides apart so the tail sits up.

Arrange shrimp on large baking pan. Season with salt and pepper; sprinkle very lightly with paprika. Set aside.

Preheat oven to 500 degrees. Place shrimp in oven and bake 5 to 6 minutes, until shrimp turn pink (do not overcook). Warm six plates.

Scampi Butter
- 2 pounds soft margarine
- ¾ cup fresh ground garlic
- ½ cup freshly squeezed lemon juice
- 6 to 8 ice cubes

In blender or food processor, whip the margarine, garlic and lemon juice to a creamy consistency. Add ice cubes; whip until the mixture rises to the top of the blender. Transfer to a saucepan and melt slowly over extremely low heat as the shrimp are cooking. Do not boil or overheat or the butter will separate.

Arrange 6 cooked shrimp with tails in the air on each warmed dinner plate. Spoon several spoonfuls of the Scampi Butter over each serving. Garnish with chopped parsley and serve immediately.

Serves 6.

Veal Scallopini al Marsala

- 1 pound boneless veal, sliced into strips
- ⅓ cup all-purpose flour
- 3 tablespoons margarine
- ½ cup Marsala wine
- ½ cup water

Lightly flour veal strips on both sides. In a large frying pan, melt margarine. Add veal and saute until lightly browned. Add marsala and stir well for a few seconds. Add water and continue stirring. Cook over medium heat 30 seconds, then remove.

Serve plain or with pasta such as linguini and steamed vegetables.

Note: Chicken is an excellent substitute for the veal.

Serves 3 to 4.

Vargo's Special Fillet

- 6 (7-ounce) beef fillets
- ½ cup all-purpose flour
- Salt and pepper as needed
- 4 tablespoons margarine
- 1 medium onion, diced
- 1 pound fresh mushrooms, sliced
- 3 tablespoons fresh lemon juice

Season flour to taste with salt and pepper. Lightly flour fillets. In a large frying pan, melt 2 tablespoons margarine and saute fillets to desired doneness. Remove from pan, set aside and keep warm.

For sauce, melt remaining margarine in same pan. Add onion and saute until clear. Add mushrooms and lemon juice. Season to taste. Saute until mushrooms are cooked. Serve over fillets.

The chef suggests serving the veal with fresh asparagus.

Serves 6.

Chicken alla Romana

- 6 (8-ounce) boneless, skinless chicken breasts
- 1 pound fresh pasta (preferably fettucini), cooked
- 1 cup extra-virgin olive oil
- 3 green bell peppers, chopped
- 3 medium onions, peeled and chopped
- 10 peeled tomatoes or 1 (16-ounce) can tomatoes (preferably Progresso)
- 1 (6-ounce) can tomato paste (preferably Contadina)
- 1 tablespoon crushed oregano
- 4 garlic cloves, mashed and chopped
- ½ cup fresh chopped basil
- ½ cup all-purpose flour
- ¼ cup margarine
- Chopped parsley for garnish

Cook fettucini while preparing chicken and sauce. Drain well before serving.

For sauce, heat ½ cup olive oil in large frying pan. Add peppers and onions and saute until onions are clear. Add tomatoes, tomato paste, oregano, garlic and basil. Stir well and cook over medium heat 15 to 20 minutes, stirring constantly. Add remaining olive oil. Cook another 5 minutes. Remove from heat, cover and set aside.

Lightly flour chicken on both sides. Melt margarine in large frying pan and saute chicken until each piece is well browned on both sides. Remove and cut each breast into 4 strips.

Place 4 pieces of chicken on each plate on top of pasta. Scoop the sauce over each serving and garnish with chopped parsley.

Serves 6.

Diet Alert: Use non-stick pan and spray with non-stick spray to saute vegetables; reduce olive oil to ½ cup or less. Reduce margarine to 2 tablespoons and saute chicken in non-stick pan.

Vargo's Chocolate Roll

- 8 eggs, separated
- Powdered sugar
- 1½ ounces (about 3 tablespoons) unsweetened cocoa powder
- 1 teaspoon vanilla
- ½ cup whipping cream
- 1 tablespoon sugar
- ¼ teaspoon vanilla

Beat egg yolks until smooth with 3 ounces (about ½ cup) powdered sugar, cocoa and vanilla. Set aside.

Beat egg whites until very stiff. Fold into yolk mixture. Line a well-greased 16x12-inch flat pan or jellyroll pan with parchment or wax paper. Grease paper. Pour in batter and bake 10 to 15 minutes at 350 degrees.

Dust a hand towel lightly with sifted powdered sugar. Remove chocolate roll from oven and turn out onto towel.

While chocolate roll cools, beat whipping cream with sugar and vanilla until smooth. Do not overbeat. For best results, chill cream, bowl and beaters thoroughly before beating.

Lightly spread cream on chocolate roll and roll up from the long side. Refrigerate until chilled.

To serve, slice roll and place one slice on plate, spoon chocolate syrup over each slice and sprinkle with chopped almonds.

Makes 8 to 10 servings.

Vargo's
2401 Fondren
Houston, Texas 77063
782-3888

Special helps

Some terms and recipes from restaurant owners and professional chefs may be unfamiliar to the home cook. Here are several that you may see frequently.

Blue cornmeal — Typical New Mexican ingredient used in Southwestern cooking, blue cornmeal provides distinctive taste and color. See Shopping Guide for some local sources. Also may be ordered from Williams-Sonoma.

Brown Sauce (Sauce Espagnole) — One of the foundation or "mother" sauces of French cooking, the base for many other sauces. Here is an easy recipe.

- 2 tablespoons oil
- 1 small onion, finely chopped
- 1 tablespoon finely chopped fresh parsley
- ½ carrot, grated
- Pinch of dried thyme
- 1 bay leaf
- 1½ tablespoons flour
- 1½ cups beef stock or bouillon (see Beef Stock recipe that follows, use canned or 1 teaspoon instant bouillon granules dissolved in 1½ cups boiling water)
- Salt and pepper as needed

Heat oil in a large skillet. Add onion, parsley, carrot, thyme and bay leaf.

Stir in flour and simmer slowly until browned, about 10 minutes. Whisk in stock. season to taste (don't over-salt) and simmer about 2 minutes. Strain.

Capers — the small green berry-like buds of the caper bush used as a condiment or to give piquant flavor to sauces. Usually available bottled or pickled in vinegar.

Clarified butter — Often used in delicate, fine dishes because it doesn't burn as easily as whole butter. Melt butter (preferably unsalted) over low heat until the foam disappears from top and sediment collects in bottom of pan. Butter should be golden yellow and clear; do not let burn. Pour clear butter off; discard sediment.

Cream — When chefs talk about cream, they usually mean heavy cream (36 percent milkfat). Heavy cream is usually labeled whipping cream. When whipped, it doubles in volume. Most whipping cream now is ultra-pasteurized for longer shelf life. Better texture and optimum volume are achieved if the cream, bowl and beaters are thoroughly chilled before the cream is beaten. A few better supermarkets stock heavy whipping cream.

If light cream is specified, look for cream labeled coffee cream or table cream.

Deglaze — Pour off all but a tablespoon or two of accumulated fat from sauteed food. Add stock, water, wine or liquid called for in the recipe and simmer, scraping up browned bits from bottom of pan with a wooden spoon.

Diet alert — In this cookbook, substitutions have been suggested in many recipes. In others, which are obviously high-fat or high-calorie, substitutions have not been suggested because portions were controlled, because we felt taste or the integrity of the recipe was affected — or because the indulgence is worth it.

Most nutrition experts and health organizations currently advocate the 50-30-20 diet — 50 percent of calories from carbohydrate, 30 percent or less from fat and 20 percent from protein.

Carbohydrates should be complex carbohydrates such as fresh vegetables, fruits, grains and beans, not refined carbohydrates. Recommended fat guidelines are that of the 30 percent, 10 percent should come from polyunsaturated fat, less than 10 percent from saturated fat and the rest from monounsaturated fats such as olive oil.

Check labels carefully for nutritional analysis of products.

Low-fat low-sodium cheeses, non-fat yogurt, skim milk and canned evaporated skim milk, egg substitute, sugar substitute, light cream cheese, light mayonnaise and salad dressing, soft tub margarine and diet margarine may often be substituted for higher fat, higher calorie ingredients without markedly affecting taste.

End Hunger Network — Many of the hotels and restaurants in this book contribute unused food to the End Hunger Network, a worldwide alliance of private and volunteer organizations committed to ending hunger in the world by the year 2000.

The Houston Chapter sponsors the Red Barrel program of food collection in hundreds of local supermarkets and the End Hunger Loop, which collects food from restaurants and distributes it to area missions and shelters. Call 963-0099 for information.

Herbs — Fresh are preferable if of good quality. They are increasingly easier to find in Houston supermarkets. The rule of thumb in substituting dried herbs is one to three — one teaspoon dried substituted for three teaspoons fresh.

Lemon zest — thinnest yellow part of the peel only.

Olive oil — Extra-virgin olive oil is preferred by most chefs because it is the finest quality and has a more delicate flavor. Because it has a low smoking point, it is not suitable for frying as are lower grades. Use extra-virgin olive oil for salad dressings or uncooked dishes.

Less expensive grades such as superfine virgin, virgin or those labeled "pure" are better for everyday use. Store olive oil in a cool, dark place.

Pasta — Make your own or purchase from supermarkets or pasta shops; use fresh or dried. Fresh pasta is best with light, fresh tomato sauces or delicate cream sauces; dried pasta, with heartier long-simmered meat and red sauces.

Fresh pasta takes only 3 to 5 minutes to cook; dried may take as long as 15. Pasta should always be cooked "al dente" which means "firm to the tooth". It should lose its floury taste, but not be hard or mushy. Do not rinse cooked pasta with cold water unless using pasta for salads.

Peppers — To roast bell peppers, rinse and dry, place on baking sheet and broil 4 to 5 inches from heat 5 minutes on each side or until the surface of each pepper is blistered and somewhat blackened. Drop into ice water and let sit for a few minutes; skins will rub off easily.

Other methods: Rub peppers with oil (optional) and grill over mesquite or charcoal, or place on end of long-tined fork and hold over gas burner until charred. Proceed as above to peel.

Handle jalapenos and other hot peppers with care as peppers and fumes can irritate skin and eyes. Wearing rubber gloves is recommended. Removing the walls and seeds of peppers cuts the heat.

Reduce — Cook a mixture down slowly until reduced by half or amount specified. In contemporary cooking, reductions are frequently used to concentrate flavors or thicken sauces instead of thickening with flour.

Roux — A mixture of flour and fat that is the thickening base for many sauces and soups, particularly Cajun dishes such as gumbo. The usual method is to heat oil until it is at the point of smoking, then to whisk in flour and stir constantly until mixture is a dark mahogany brown, almost black.

Roux requires close attention; it must be stirred or whisked almost constantly for 45 minutes to an hour or it will burn.

Roux is much easier in the microwave. The following method is described by newspaper microwave columnists Ann Steiner and CiCi Williamson in their first book, "Microwave Know-How."

Heat ½ cup each oil and flour in a 4-cup glass measure. Microwave on high power 6 to 7 minutes, stirring every minute after 4 minutes, until a deep brown roux is formed.

Stock — Stocks made on the premises are the rule with chefs of restaurants represented in this book, but most realize that busy home cooks will use canned broth and stocks. Unfortunately, canned broths tend to be very salty so choose low-sodium canned broth or buy good quality canned products and adjust salt called for in the recipe.

When making stock at home, use a non-aluminum pan. For clear stock, skim foam and scum off top as it accumulates. Stir as little as possible to prevent clouding. Stock should simmer slowly, not boil. Cool quickly (setting the pan of stock in a container or sink or cold water speeds the process).

Chill, then remove congealed fat from top. Refrigerate or freeze.

Beef stock: Combine 2 to 4 pounds beef bones and meaty soup bones and trimmings (brown half the meat) in a saucepot. Add 3 quarts cold water, 8 peppercorns, 1 each onion, carrot and celery rib cut in pieces, 3 whole cloves, 1 bay leaf, 5 sprigs parsley and other desired herbs such as dried thyme.

Bring to a boil and skim off foam. Simmer covered 3 hours, skimming occasionally. Strain stock, cool quickly and refrigerate or freeze. When cold, remove any solid fat that has risen to the top. (Remove fat before freezing.)

Chicken stock: Place 3 pounds bony chicken parts in a stockpot with 3 quarts cold water, a quartered onion stuck with 2 whole cloves, 2 each celery ribs and carrots, 10 peppercorns, 5 sprigs parsley and 1 bay leaf. Cover pot, bring to a boil over medium heat, then reduce heat and simmer stock partially covered, 2 to 3 hours.

For a clear stock, skim off foam and scum that collects on the surface. Add salt to taste after about 1 hour. Strain stock and discard bones and solids. Let cool. Refrigerate or freeze when cool.

Fish stock: Follow method for chicken stock above using 2 pounds fish bones, heads and tails, half the amount of onion, celery and carrots, 6 peppercorns and 1 cup dry white wine if desired. Fish stock needs to be simmered uncovered only about 30 minutes, until reduced by half. Longer simmering may produce off tastes. Skim while simmering. Let cool uncovered. When cool, refrigerate or freeze.

Vinegar — Use clear white vinegar unless another type, such as cider, fruit-flavored, rice wine or balsamic vinegar is specified. **Balsamic vinegar,** a dark, aged Italian vinegar that is very popular with food professionals and the gourmet cooks, especially in salad dressings.

Shopping Guide

Here are some sources for gourmet ingredients called for in recipes in "Houston Gourmet Cooks 2."

Better supermarkets carry most items including cilantro (fresh coriander or Chinese parsley), fresh produce such as tomatillos, spices, herbs, puff pastry, imported sauces and fish.

Bakeries such as French Gourmet on Westheimer and Paris Bakery in Clear lake at 515 Bay Area Boulevard and 8405 Winkler near South Houston sell puff pastry dough, patty shells and specialty breads

General

Fiesta Marts, 15 locations; check the Yellow Pages or call 869-5060 for location nearest you. Excellent source for fresh produce, baked goods, specialty foods and imported items from all over the world, especially Mexican, Latin, Chinese, Asian and Middle Eastern.

Fiesta's largest market, 110,000 square feet, is at Bellaire Boulevard and Hillcroft. At Bellaire Boulevard and Highway 6 is a 75,000-square-foot store which has the ambiance of a Mexican mercado. It features specialty baked goods, carry-out Japanese sushi, fajitas and exotic fresh produce from all over the world. One of the newest stores is at San Jacinto and Wheeler; it serves the downtown and near Southwest areas including Montrose and West University Place. An 80,000-square-foot store is scheduled to open in October '88 at Kirby and Old Spanish Trail across from the Astrodome.

Jamail Family Market, 3333 S. Rice Avenue, south of The Galleria area. This newcomer among specialty food shops which opened in May, 1987, is operated by brother and sister, Joe Jamail and Marian Jamail Averyt, and Joe's sons, Jimmy and Larry — part of the family known as "the" gourmet food merchants of Houston. (Setting for color photograph on back cover of cookbook.)

They pride themselves on stocking the freshest and finest produce, meats and seafood and wines. Selections reflect customers favorites. The bakery features custom desserts by Jeanne Kalil Hemwattakit. The gourmet deli, overseen by Michele Yamin, specializes in light cuisine including fat-and sodium-reduced entrees and salads. 621-8030.

Jim Jamail and Sons, 3114 Kirby Dr. in the River Oaks area. Houston's gourmet food store of record. Full lines of imported and domestic cheeses, fresh fruits and vegetables, fresh herbs, excellent meats and fish, low-cholesterol, low-sodium items, imported sauces, seasonings and condiments, wines, pastas, chocolates, baked goods, coffees, teas and wines.

Jamail Brothers Food Market, Clarence & Edward. 2110 S. Shepherd. 523-5535. Small, but select. Personal attention and fine quality are the tradition here.

Jumbo Supermarkets, 9750 Fondren, 10250 Westheimer and West Columbia, Texas. Good source for Chinese, Asian, Mexican, Middle Eastern and Cajun ingredients including fresh produce and sauces.

Kroger store at 3664 Highway 6 at Settler's Way in Sugar Land. Opened in May, 1988, this 62,000-square-foot supermarket is an example of the new "Power Alley" supermarket concept. Heavy emphasis is placed on specialty perishable items and gourmet foods—a wine steward is in charge of what Kroger boasts is the largest selection of wines in a Texas supermarket, and there are more than 400 varieties of produce including a large section of imported and ethnic items. In-house fruit and vegetable juice bar; wide selection of cheeses, gourmet cooking oils and vinegars. Deli includes specialties prepared by in-house chef.

Leibman's, 14014A Memorial Dr. at Kirkwood. 493-3663. Excellent source for wines, spices such as hard-to-find saffron, large selections of Southwestern ingredients—dried chilies, basil pesto mix, blue corn meal—extra-virgin olive oils, vinegars (including McLean's loganberry and raspberry vinegars from Washington State), rices, pastas, specialty bacons and meats such as pancetta, air-dried beef (Italian brasola and German buenderfleisch) and double smoked bacon, prosciutto, deboned quail, dried mushrooms, mustards (42 varieties), olives, chutneys, condiments, sun-dried tomatoes (bulk and in oil), creme fraiche and cheeses including Larsen's goat milk cheese from Texas and Fine Forme low-fat, reduced salt and low-cholesterol (.008 gram per one ounce).

Randall's Flagship stores, three locations—1407 South Voss Road at Woodway; 5586 Weslayan at Bissonnet, and 5219 FM 1960 in Champions. Superior supermarkets featuring imported and locally grown fresh produce, domestic and imported specialty foods, meats and seafood. Will custom-order products on request.

Rice Epicurean Market, 5016 San Felipe—remodeled and expanded in 1988, it is now one of the city's finest specialty gourmet stores. Michael Bove, specialty foods director, and buyers have assembled "boutique" collections of gourmet foods including regional and ethnic items, cheeses, wines, meats, seafood, pastas, oils, vinegars, chocolates, deli and imported foods. A full kitchen provides gourmet take-out items and there's an in-house butcher and bakery.

Star attractions: Texas specialty foods, Fini dried and fresh pastas and frozen entrees from Italy, Wolfgang Puck pizzas and frozen desserts, ice creams (exclusive Houston outlet for Double Rainbow of San Francisco and Ben & Jerry's Peace Pop).

Richard's Liquors and Fine Wines—2124 S. Shepherd and several locations including the newest on Memorial in Lantern Lane Shopping Center. Richard's was established in 1949 and continues to be one of the city's finest wine and food specialty shops.

Star attractions: wines from around the world including great vintages and large selections of French Bordeaux and Burgundies; exclusive local source for award-winning Stag's Leap wines from California; extensive line of imported and domestic cheeses including Texas goat cheeses from Fredericksburg and caciotta from Dallas; extensive line of imported and domestic deli meats including Italian pancetta bacon, prosciutto, Westphalian and Black Forest hams; custom gift baskets; series of wine seminars/tastings; wide selection of specialty Cognacs, brandies, fruit brandies and Scotches.

Spec's Liquor Warehouse & Deli, 2410 Smith Street. Also Spec's at 1029 Bay Area Blvd. in Clear Lake and 14625 Memorial at Dairy Ashford. Vast selection of wines, liquors and liqueurs, coffee (more than 80 varieties including La Minita Tarrazu, a Costa Rican coffee that rivals Jamaican; most of the beans are roasted in-house), domestic and imported cheeses (including aged American and Danish blues, English blue Cheddar and Valembert, which is like a low-fat Brie), spices and seasonings, oils (including Soleillou, a French pimiento oil), unique pastas (including the Di Ceo line from Arizona), preserves, vinegars, dried tomatoes and several varieties of dried mushrooms.

Whole Foods Market, 2900 S. Shepherd. Imported and/or organically grown fruits and vegetables, sauces, condiments, wide variety of bulk grains and cereals, spices and seasonings, cheeses, natural yogurts, frozen foods, additive-free beef and chicken, baked goods, wines, beers, teas, coffees.

Williams-Sonoma, 4076 Westheimer (622-4161) and 30 Town & Country center (465-4775). Sauces, condiments, blue cornmeal, herbs de provence and own line of dry spices, Anaheim chilies, Martelli pasta, professional vanilla, Callebaut and confiture chocolate (white, chips and dipping chocolate), strings of chilies and garlic, bay leaf wreaths, olive oils (including a new one, Travigne, pressed from California Mission olives) and vinegars including Fini balsamic vinegar from Italy.

CHINESE, ASIAN

Various markets in Chinatown east of Main Street around McKinney and St. Emanuel.

Asiatic Import Company, 909 Chartres (227-7979).

Chinatown Market, 1806 Polk Ave. (650-0757).

Diho Market, 9280 Bellaire Blvd. (988-1881). Extensive stock of Chinese and Oriental products, fresh meats, fish, wines, sauces, frozen and prepared items.

Dynasty Supermarket in Dynasty Plaza, 9600 Bellaire (995-4088). Full line supermarket of Oriental and Chinese staples, condiments and hot deli items; fresh fish, wines and beers.

Korea Super Market, 6427 Bissonnet, 772-6160.

Daido Japanese Market, Westheimer at Wilcrest (785-0815).

INDIAN

Jay Stores, 6688 Southwest Fwy.
Patel Brothers, 6822 Harwin.
Both have a full line of Indian ingredients and products, spices and condiments; some Asian products.

VIETNAMESE

Saigon Supermarket, 10815 Beechnut at Wilcrest.
Crystal Palace on Milam.
Hoa Nam, 8282 Bellaire.
Vietnam Plaza, 2200 Jefferson, 222-6280.
Viet Hoa Supermarket, 8200 Wilcrest at Beechnut, 561-8706. In the process of expanding, this is a complete supermarket, fish market and produce shop.

Index

APPETIZERS
Austin's Seafood Stuffed Mushrooms (Austin's) 25
Avocado Mousse With Crab and Dijon Vinaigrette (Anthony's) 13
Avocado Shrimp With Tangy and Spicy Sauce (Empress of China) 37
Ceviche (Tony Mandola's) 95
Cheese Spread (Vargo's) 97
Deviled Crab/Crab Balls (Tony Mandola's) 94
Eggplant Terrine (Tony's) 89
Ground Pork Appetizer (Nam Sodd-Thai Cafe) 85
Karbar Beef Strings (Empress of China) 38
Mexican Pizza (Cafe Adobe) 24
Roasted Poblano Crab Cakes With Lemon Caper Tomato Mayonnaise (Prego) 65
Salted Crabs With Black Pepper (Kim Son) 46
Satay With Peanut Butter Sauce and Cucumber Salad (Thai Cafe) 85
Shrimp Cocktail Vicente (Tony Mandola's) 93
Shrimp With Wild Mushrooms and Fresh Noodles (La Tour d'Argent) 54
Smoked Lamb Nachos, Poached Tortilla Chips, Refried Black Beans
  and Pico de Gallo (DeVille-Four Seasons) .... 31 & 32
Spinach With Mozzarella Cheese (Cavatore) 27
Spring Rolls (Kim Son) 46

BEVERAGES
Cafe Cavatore 29
Earl Grey Sour (Les Continents/The Brasserie) 57
Kiwi Ginger Sparkle (Les Continents/The Brasserie) 57
Thai Tea (Thai Cafe) 87
Vietnamese Coffee (Kim Son) 47

BREADS
Seven Grain Bread (DeVille-Four Seasons Hotel) 35
Zucchini Nut Bread (Rudi Lechner's) 83

CHICKEN AND POULTRY
Chicken
Baby Chicken Framboise (Tony's) 90
Baby Chicken Mercado With Cilantro Lime Butter (Les Continents/The Brasserie) 58
Breast of Chicken With Peppercorns (Tony's) 90
Breast of Chicken With Rosemary (Cavatore) 28
Chicken alla Romana (Vargo's) 99
Chicken Breast Southern California (Rudi Lechner's) 82
Chicken Taco Salad (Cafe Adobe) 23
Chicken With Green Asparagus Coulis (La Reserve-Inn on the Park) 50
Chinese Chicken Salad With Honey Ginger Dressing (Quail Hollow Inn) 69
Crepe Hubert (Rudi Lechner's) 82
Four Delight of Kung Pao (Hunan River) 41
Grilled Chicken Caesar Salad (The Remington) 79
Grilled Chicken Salad (Prego) 66
Involtini de Pollo (Rao's Ristorante Italiano & Bar) 74
Peking Roasted Chicken (Empress of China) 39
Sand on the Snow (Empress of China) 39
South of the Border Fettucini With Grilled Chicken and Black Beans (Prego) 66
Pheasant With Dried Apricots and Cream Sauce (La Tour d'Argent) 53

Quail With Apples (Quail Hollow Inn) 70
Stir-Fried Duck With Oriental Vegetables and Sesame Pasta (The Remington) 77

DESSERTS
Apple Tart (Tony's) 91
Bananas (Flamed, Martinique-Style) — La Tour d'Argent 55
Cheesecake
     Blueberry Cheesecake (Louisiana Don's) 63
     Cheesecake (Quail Hollow Inn) 71
     Strawberry Cheesecake (Les Continents/The Brasserie) 59
Chocolate Roll (Vargo's) 99
Cobbler of Peaches, Basil and Cherries With
  Southern Comfort Sauce (DeVille-Four Seasons Hotel) 34
Glazed Strawberry Dessert Soup (Les Continents/The Brasserie) 59
Lemon Tart (La Reserve-Inn on the Park) 51
Louisiana Meringue Bread Pudding (Louisiana Don's) 63
Sopabananapilla (Cafe Adobe) 24
Sticky Rice and Mango (Thai Cafe) 87
Tony Mandola's Bread Puddin' With Whiskey Sauce (Tony Mandola's) 95
White Chocolate Mousse (Anthony's) 15
Pies
     Austin's Texas Brownie Pie (Austin's) 25
     Mile High Mud Pie With Warm Chocolate Sauce (Brennan's) 21

FISH AND SEAFOOD
Austin's Seafood Stuffed Mushrooms (Austin's) 25
Campfire Salmon (DeVille-Four Seasons Hotel) 32
Ceviche (Tony Mandola's) 95
Crab
     Avocado Mousse With Crab and Dijon Vinaigrette (Anthony's) 13
     Deviled Crab/Crab Balls (Tony Mandola's) 94
     Maryland She Crab Soup (The Remington) 77
     Roasted Poblano Crab Cakes With Lemon Caper Tomato Mayonnaise (Prego) 65
     Salted Crabs With Black Pepper (Kim Son) 46
Crawfish Etouffee (Louisiana Don's) 61
Fettucini Pescatore (Cavatore) 27
Flounder (Poached, With Peppercorn Cream Sauce) — La Reserve-Inn on the Park 50
Flounder With Lime (Quail Hollow Inn) 70
Lemon Sole With Mustard, Breadcrumbs, Chives, Tomatoes and Basil (Anthony's) 14
Redfish (Fillet of, Wrapped in Lettuce Leaves) — Les Continents/The Brasserie 57
Scallops
     Four Delight of Kung Pao (Hunan River) 41
     Sesame Scallops (Empress of China) 38
     Steamed Scallops and Vegetables (Hunan River) 41
     Veal and Sea Scallops Bianchina (Cavatore) 29
Shrimp
     Avocado Shrimp With Tangy and Spicy Sauce (Empress of China) 37
     Gratin of Shrimp With Wild Mushrooms and Fresh Noodles (La Tour d'Argent) ... 54
     Four Delight of Kung Pao (Hunan River) 41
     Gulf Shrimp With Crispy Rice Cakes and Creole Meuniere Sauce (Brennan's) 18
     Imperial Two Flavors (Hunan River) 42
     Quail Hunters Delicacy (Quail Hollow Inn) 71
     Shrimp and Avocado Salad (Louisiana Don's) 62
     Shrimp Cocktail Vicente (Tony Mandola's) 93

    Shrimp Enchiladas With Ranchero Sauce (Cafe Adobe) 23
    Shrimp Fried Rice (Hunan River/Red Pepper) 42
    Shrimp Scampi (Vargo's) 98
    Shrimp With Wild Mushrooms and Fresh Noodles (La Tour d'Argent) 54
Seafood Lasagna (Tony Mandola's) 94
Snapper
    Seared Gulf Red Snapper With Mint Marigold Sauce and Three Salsas (The Remington) .. 78
    Snapper Courtbouillon (Louisiana Don's) 61
    Snapper Toto (Rao's Ristorante Italiano & Bar) 74
Swordfish Salad (Tony's) 89
Tuna (Fresh Grilled, Salad) — Brennan's 19

MEAT
Beef
    Austin's Meatloaf (Austin's) 25
    Beef Tenderloin on a Bed of Sweet Onions With Creole Mustard Sauce (Brennan's) 19
    Beef Tenderloin Tips in Green Peppercorn Cream Sauce With
        Garlic Fried Rice (Les Continents/The Brasserie) 58
    Beef With Sweet Basil (Thai Cafe) 86
    Braciole alla Napoletana (Tony's) 91
    Calf Liver With Red Onion-Apple Butter Sauce (Rudi Lechner's) 83
    Charcoal Broiled Beef With Lemon Grass (Kim Son) 47
    Four Delight of Kung Pao 41
    Imperial Two Flavors (Hunan River) 42
    Karbar Beef Strings (Empress of China) 38
    Satay With Peanut Butter Sauce and Cucumber Salad (Thai Cafe) 85
    Vargo's Special Filet 98
Charcoaled Axis Venison With Red Bell Pepper Sauce (DeVille-Four Seasons Hotel) 33
Four Delight of Kung Pao (Hunan River) 41
Lamb
    Grilled Lamb Chops With Pink Peppercorn Sauce (Prego) 67
    Medallions of Lamb With Three Mushrooms and Basil Sauce
        (La Reserve-Inn on the Park) 51
Pork
    Cajun Stuffed Pork Roast (Louisiana Don's) 62
    Ground Pork Appetizer (Nam Sodd-Thai Cafe) 85
Veal
    Veal and Scallops Bianchina (Cavatore) 29
    Veal Medallions With Endive and Ginger (La Tour d'Argent) 54
    Veal Pancetta With Mascarpone and Pancetta Sauce (Anthony's) 14
    Veal Scallopini (Vargo's) 98

PASTA/RICE
Pasta
    Fettucini (Fresh, With Gratin of Shrimp) — La Tour d'Argent 54
    Fettucini Pescatore (Cavatore) 27
    Green and White Pasta Primavera (Anthony's) 13
    Ravioli al Sugo (Rao's Ristorante Italiano & Bar) 75
    South of the Border Fettucini With Grilled Chicken and Black Beans (Prego) 66
    Summery Linguini With Black Beans, Corn, Cilantro and Tomato Sauce for Two (Prego) .. 67
Rice
    Crispy Rice Cakes (With Gulf Shrimp) — Brennan's 18
    Garlic Fried Rice (Les Continents/The Brasserie) 58
    Red Beans, Rice and Sausage (Tony Mandola's) 93

    Shrimp Fried Rice (Hunan River/Red Pepper) 42
    Sticky Rice and Mango Dessert (Thai Cafe) 87
    Tony Rao's Risotto (Rao's Ristorante Italiano & Bar) 73

SALADS/SALAD DRESSINGS
Chicken
    Chicken Taco Salad (Cafe Adobe) 23
    Chinese Chicken Salad With Honey Ginger Dressing (Quail Hollow Inn) 69
    Grilled Chicken Caesar Salad (The Remington) 79
    Grilled Chicken Salad (Prego) 66
Cucumber Salad (With Satay) — Thai Cafe 85
Curly Endive With Goat Cheese (La Tour d'Argent) 54
Grilled Fresh Tuna Salad (Brennan's) 19
Low-Cal Green Apple and Jicama Slaw (DeVille-Four Seasons Hotel) 33
Papaya Salad (Thai Cafe) 86
Radicchio and Fennel Salad (Rao's Ristorante Italiano & Bar) 73
Shrimp and Avocado Salad (Louisiana Don's) 62
Spring Salad With Boursin Wontons (La Reserve-Inn on the Park) 49
Swordfish Salad (Tony's) 89
Tomatoes Anthony With Pecan Vinaigrette Dressing (Anthony's) 12
Warm Spinach Salad With Pancetta Bacon and Sherry Vinaigrette (The Remington) 79

SAUCES, MARINADES, SEASONING
Basil Sauce With Medallions of Lamb (La Reserve-Inn on the Park) 51
Brown Sauce (see Special Helps section) 100
Creole Meuniere Sauce (With Gulf Shrimp With Crispy Rice Cakes) — Brennan's 18
Creole Mustard Sauce (With Beef Tenderloin on a Bed of Sweet Onions) — Brennan's 19
Dijon Vinaigrette (With Avocado Mousse With Crab) — Anthony's 13
Lasagna Sauce for Seafood Lasagna (Tony Mandola's) 94
Lemon Caper Tomato Mayonnaise (With Roasted Poblano Crab Cakes) — Prego 65
Marinade for cooking duck (The Remington) 77
Marinade for Spring Salad With Boursin Wontons (La Reserve-Inn on the Park) 49
Marinara Sauce (With Eggplant Parmesan) — Cavatore 28
Mascarpone and Pancetta Sauce With Veal Pancetta (Anthony's) 14
Mint Marigold Sauce (With Seared Gulf Red Snapper) — The Remington 78
Mousseline Sauce (With Asparagus) — La Tour d'Argent 55
Peanut Butter Sauce (With Satay) — Thai Cafe 85
Pecan Vinaigrette Dressing (With Tomatoes Anthony) — Anthony's 12
Peppercorn Cream Sauce (With Poached Flounder) — La Reserve (Inn on the Park) ... 50
Ranchero Sauce (Cafe Adobe) 23
Red Bell Pepper Sauce (With Axis Venison) — DeVille-Four Seasons Hotel 33
Dessert
    Southern Comfort Sauce (With Cobbler of Peaches) — DeVille Four Seasons Hotel 35
    Warm Chocolate Sauce (With Mile High Mud Pie) — Brennan's 21
    Whiskey Sauce for Bread Puddin' (Tony Mandola's) 95
Salsas
    Jicama Tomatillo Salsa (The Remington) 78
    Mango Black Bean Salsa (The Remington) 79
    Pico de Gallo (DeVille-Four Seasons Hotel) 32
    Yellow Bell Pepper Tomato Salsa (The Remington) 78

SOUP
Chilled Artichoke Soup (La Reserve-Inn on the Park) 49
Cucumber Dill Soup (Anthony's) 11
Glazed Strawberry Dessert Soup (Les Continents/The Brasserie) 59

Jalapeno Cheese Soup (Brennan's)	17
Maryland She Crab Soup (The Remington)	77
Stocks — Beef, Chicken and Fish (see Special Helps section)	101 & 102
Thai Coconut Chicken Soup (Thom Ka Gai) — Thai Cafe	86
White Wine Cheese Soup (Rudi Lechner's)	81

VEGETABLES

Asparagus With Mousseline Sauce (La Tour d'Argent)	55
Austin's Seafood Stuffed Mushrooms	25
Broccoli in Garlic Sauce (Hunan River)	43
Broccoli in Special Garlic Sauce (Empress of China)	38
Creole Succotash Timbales (Brennan's)	20
Dry Sauteed String Beans (Hunan River/Red Pepper)	43
Eggplant Parmesan With Marinara Sauce (Cavatore)	28
Eggplant Terrine (Tony's)	89
Red Beans and Rice With Sausage (Tony Mandola's)	93
Refried Black Beans (With Smoked Lamb Nachos) — DeVille-Four Seasons Hotel	31
Spinach With Mozzarella (Cavatore)	27
Stir-Fried Vegetables (Thai Cafe)	87

About Ann Criswell

Ann Criswell, who has been food editor of the *Houston Chronicle* since 1966, has also written freelance food articles, authored three cookbooks and edited several others.

As food editor of the Chronicle, she contributed most of the recipes in the "Texas the Beautiful Cookbook" published in October, 1986.

She is a member of the Newspaper Food Editors and Writers Association, International Food Media Conference, the Houston Culinary Guild and the Spring, Texas, chapter of the Chaine des Rotisseurs.

In 1987 she was named the first honorary member of the South Texas Dietetic Association. She has received awards of excellence from the American Heart Association, American Cancer Society and Texas Restaurant Association. In 1988 she was named the first honoree of the Texas Chefs Association.

Because of a special interest in wine, she has made several wine tours in Europe and California and has judged Texas wine competitions. She has also judged national cooking contests including the National Beef Cook-Off, National Chicken Cooking Contest and America's Bake-Off.

She is a graduate of Texas Woman's University. Her late husband was a Houston newspaperman and she has a daughter, Catherine, 26, and son, Charles, 24.

Who's Who Houston Gourmet Cooks 2

Top Row (Left to right)
Sonny Lahham - La Tour d'Argent ★ Kaspar Donier - La Reserve-Inn on the Park ★ Michael Sadek - Cavatore ★ Ann Criswell - Food Editor Houston Chronicle ★ Jody Larriviere - Louisiana Don's ★ Tony Mandola - Tony Mandola's ★ Brian Drennan - Prego ★ Helmut Sussenbach - Les Continents/The Brasserie Hotel Inter-Continental ★ Scott Chen - Empress of China ★ Tony Rao - Rao's ★ Guiseppe Briguglio - Vargo's ★

Bottom Row (Left to right)
Wen Lee - Hunan River ★ Tony Ruppe - DeVille-Four Seasons-Houston Center ★ Fran Fauntleroy - Publisher ★ Mark Cox - Tony's ★ Karl Camenzind - Quail Hollow Inn ★ Peter Rosenberg - The Remington on Post Oak Park ★

HOUSTON GOURMET COOKS 2

Order a book for a friend.
A Perfect Gift

ORDER FORM

For additional copies of this cookbook contact:
HOUSTON GOURMET
2 Pine Forest
Houston, Texas 77056

Please mail me _____ copies of your **HOUSTON GOURMET COOKS 2** at $12.95 per copy plus $2.00 handling and postage per book. Texas residents, also add applicable state sales tax. Enclosed is my check or money order for $ _____ .

Mail books to:

Name _____

Address _____

City/State _____ Zip _____

OTHER BOOKS AVAILABLE

___ **HOUSTON GOURMET COOKS**
A Collection of Recipes from 21 of Houston's Most Creative Restaurants. $12.95

___ **HOUSTON GOURMET 88**
The Ultimate Menu Guide to Fine Dining in the Houston Area $6.95

Please include $2.00 per book for handling & postage. Texas residents, also add applicable state sales tax.

Enclosed is my check or money order for $ _____ . Mail books to:

Name _____

Address _____

City/State _____ Zip _____